Cyber Security Research

Norwich University Applied Research Institutes

2016 Annual Report
Of
Top Cyber Security Incidents

Edited by:

THOMAS HYSLIP

ROSEMARIE PELLETIER

GEORGE SILOWASH

i

CONTENTS

IN MEMORY OF LARS NIELSON

COVER DESIGN

Jan Paolo Cruz

POW Graphix Unlimited

Janpaolocruzrn@yahoo.com

1

INTRODUCTION

2016 will be remembered as the year the Russians hacked the U.S. Presidential election. However, the year's cyber security incidents were much more than the information operation wage by the Russians.   As you will read in the following chapters we witnessed the first large scale Internet of Things (IOT) attack that affected a large swatch of the Internet and many significant online retailers. The National Security Agency was compromised and it's cyber weapons were used in what could have been a devastating Ransomware attack. Over 1 billion accounts were affected when Yahoo was attacked, and another 385 million MySpace accounts were compromised.

This year we examined 15 cyber security incidents. In addition to those mentioned above, we reviewed breaches at LinkedIn, Wendy's, and Uber. Both the Department of Justice and the Internal Revenue Service were attacked, as well as Verizon, MedStar Health, and Adult Friend Finder. Social networking sites

Tumblr and MySpace were compromised, and no review of 2016 would complete without examining the controversy of Secretary of State Hillary Clinton's use of a private email server.

Thank you very much for purchasing our book. The chapter authors are all current students or graduates of Norwich University, College of Graduate and Continuing Studies, Master's Degree programs.

2

2016 PRESIDENTIAL ELECTION

By: Manny Bamba and Thomas Hyslip

The Russian attacks on the US election system must be viewed and evaluated in both historical and geopolitical superpower rivalry context. In 1991, the Soviet Union was a disintegrated superpower faced with unsustainable economic woes and political conflagration. The empire was no more and many of its states had broken off. Having dueled for over 70 years with the West, led by the United States for international supremacy, the Soviet Union, now the Russian Republic strategic planners only saw this breakup and loss of prestige as temporary setbacks. So, it was only a matter of time before the Russian leadership and surviving structures would again seek to rejoin the superpower fight and attempt to defeat or reengage the West. This simple phrase by President George W. Bush at an economic summit in Abu Dhabi United Arab Emirates (USA Today, 2018) underscores this assertion " Vladimir Putin has a chip on his shoulder. The reason he does is because of the demise of the Soviet Union". This simplistic phrase by the President in reference to the Russian meddling in the US Presidential election is really the core of the opinion in the Russian "Information Warfare" on the US and by extension the WEST, in attempting to reestablish their lost leadership and prestige in the world. In effect confirming this Russian assessment, many leaders and other political entities in the West have claimed victory for the downfall of the Soviet Union as a global power, which was symbolized by the fall of the Berlin Wall that divided Germany.

Thus, the Cold War between the two superpowers had officially ended. But, the Russians became like the movies " Prizzi's honor" in the eighties when the old mob boss was told someone has stolen their money: "we forgive notin'" and went to work to reassert their former power status.

By 1993 and afterward, the traditional domains of power projections and kinetic military actions such as Land, Sea or Air by both emerging powers and superpowers along with many other actors have been expanded by the global Internet. Now the Internet reliably facilitates and enables instant communications, e-commerce, banking and financial transactions worldwide among others with huge amount of data flowing and being stored in a distributed fashion. As a result, both business and personal data are now at risk and have become targets for theft, compromise and even destruction. In this contest, the US, Russian Republic and other states and non-states actors are leveraging the Internet to launch cyber-attacks with varying attack vectors such as viruses, worms, botnet, social engineering, spear phishing or blended threats among many other cyber weapons. Advanced Persistent Threats (ATP) and opportunistic attacks have become common occurrence on the Internet landscape by organized criminal groups, script kiddies, nation states, non-state actors and other cybercriminals.

In response, new dynamic enterprises have also emerged to help governments, business and public in general to assess and mitigate these existing and emerging threats by deploying the appropriate countermeasures including providing intelligence. This panoramic view of security landscape could help us understand the context and how the Russian attacks on the US election infrastructure unfolded.

Russian Information Warfare doctrine as elaborated by Bruce McClintock a former US Defense attaché in Moscow and on Rand Corp site may have many different terminologies and methods such as "Informatsionnoye Protivoborstbo" or Information Confrontation encompassing both technical and psychological components from the Russian General Staff Academy (U.S. News & World Report; RAND blog, 2017; Airpower Journal, 1996).

Untreatably, any Information Warfare program will comprise several attack vectors or methods, targets, sectors and domains among others and the Cyber Attacks against the 2016 election certainly included multiple attack vectors and methods.

The Russian operations were first exposed in September 2015 when the FBI discovered at least one computer at the Democratic National Committee (DNC) had been compromised by Russia (CNN, 2018). Unfortunately, the DNC did not take the report seriously and made no changes or updates to their security. Again in November 2015, the FBI warned the DNC that their computers were conveying information to Russia but remarkably the DNC again took no action. It was not until June 2016, after the Washington Post reported the DNC hack that the DNC acknowledged the hack and took preventive measures (CNN, 2018).

Around the same time, Clinton campaign chairman John Podesta received a phishing email and unknowingly provided his password to hackers, who then compromised his email account (Nakashima & Harris, 2018). Podesta's email would be slowly released by WikiLeaks throughout the 2016 Presidential campaign.

The Republican National Committee (RNC) and state level organizations were also targeted by the Russian information warfare attacks, but the FBI reported only old unused email domains were compromised (Greenberg, 2017).

Subsequently these attacks were confirmed by the findings of the Cybersecurity firm Dell SecureWorks among others pointing to data theft as the employed method by the Russian intelligence services controlled or affiliated hacking group Fancy Bear. In effect, Podesta's personal Gmail account was breached thru a spear-phishing attack. This method usually consists of redirecting a user to a fake web site imitating a legitimate service provider like Gmail that a person or customer usually uses, tricking with bogus links inserted in phishing emails for example. These hacked emails ended up with Wikileaks which eventually leaked them with contents of 20,000 pages in October and November of 2016. Fancy Bear is also believed to be responsible of Cyber-attacks on both the DNC and DCCC with Wikileaks also publishing those stolen or pilfered emails as well. In executing the attacks for example, Fancy Bear sent Podesta an email on March 19, 2016 with the appearance of a google security alert message that contained a fake link intended to mislead a user to the bogus web portal set up by the hackers where the user real credentials are collected and later used to access the original or legitimate holder accounts (i.e. leveraging spear-phishing mythologies).In examining the attacks environment and the employed methods a pattern or similarities were found supporting assertions by SecureWorks that the same attack vectors had been leveraged to access Colin Powell emails in the past. In essence, the attack link had used Bitty (bitty.com) a service provider that shorten URL's to draw Podesta into logging on the fake web site and entering his Gmail account credentials which ultimately led to his account being compromised by the hackers.

Since an Information Warfare program tends to leverage multiple attack vectors and strategies, the Russians are believed to have actively used social media in impacting the 2016 Presidential Election. In this regard of wide spread attack strategies and methods, Robert Mueller, the special prosecutor in the election interference probe has issued a 37 pages indictment against 13 Russians as reported by the New York Times (Apuzzo & LaFraniere, 2018). The indictment charges them with conspiracy to defraud the United States and linked them with four year efforts to undermine and influence the 2016 Presidential Election. Furthermore, the Russians and the three companies such as Internet Research Agency, Concord Management and Concord Catering that facilitated and funded their attacks and methods are accused of using social media, identity theft of American citizens and utilizing politically charged issues and topics to manipulate the electorate in the hotly contested 2016 presidential campaign. The indictment also singled out three Russians with conspiracy to commit wire fraud and bank fraud along with five other individuals with aggravated identity theft.

In late 2017, confirming the multiple vectors and influences operations, CNN reported that Russia used Facebook ads to geographically target residents in Michigan and Wisconsin as well pose as Black Lives Matters activists on Tumblr and Pokemon Go to influence voters (CNN, 2018).

As understood, the ensuing investigations by Robert Mueller the Special Prosecutor and his team have yet to complete and present their findings as of this writing. So, the post mortem of the Russian attacks on the US presidential election and the consequences of the resulting interference have yet to be fully assessed and written to provide the lesson learned and the required mitigation process including the needed controls. However, on December 9, 2016, the CIA concluded and also told the US law makers that Russians were behind the Cyber hacks and provided the emails to Wikileaks which ultimately published them (The Guardian, 2016).

References

Apuzzo, M. and LaFraniere, S. (2018, Feb). 13 Russians Indicted as Mueller Reveals Effort to Aid Trump Campaign. New York Times. Retrieved from https://www.nytimes.com/2018/02/16/us/politics/?ussia?s-indicted-mueller-election-interference.html

Hakashima, E., & Harris, S. (2018). How the Russians hacked the DNC and passed its emails to WikiLeaks. The Washington Post. Retrieved from https://www.washingtonpost.com/world/national-security/how-the-russians-hacked-the-dnc-and-passed-its-emails-to-wikileaks/2018/07/13/af19a828-86c3-11e8-8553-a3ce89036c78_story.html?utm_term=.1050e7f9432e

CNN. (2018). 2016 Presidential Campaign Hacking Fast Facts. Retrieved from https://www.cnn.com/2016/12/26/us/2016-presidential-campaign-hacking-fast-facts/index.html

Greenberg, A. (2017, Jan). Russia hacked "older" republican emails, FBI director says. Wired. Retrieved from https://www.wired.com/2017/01/?ussia-hacked-older-republican-emails-fbi-director-says/

The Guardian. (2016, Dec 10). CIA concludes Russia interfered to help Trump win election, say reports. The Guardian. Retrieved from https://www.theguardian.com/us-news/2016/dec/10/cia-concludes-russia-interfered-to-help-trump-win-election-report

3

DEPARTMENT OF JUSTICE

By: Lyda Tesauro

In retaliation for the United States' relations with Israel, a pro-Palestinian sympathizer social engineered access to a DOJ portal, downloaded 200GB out of 1TB of data available to him, dumped a DHS staff directory with over 9,000 (almost 10,000) employee listings on Sunday, February 7, 2016, and then published 20,000 FBI employees' contact information the next day (Storm, 2016). According to CNN, the information stolen included names, titles (such as DHS PRISM Support), locations (in the U.S. and out of the country), phone numbers, and e-mail addresses (Mallonee, 2016 and Storm, 2016). The Justice Department spokesman, Peter Carr, claimed that no sensitive information (e.g. social security numbers) was obtained; however, the hacker did tell Motherboard—the technology news site that first reported the hack—that he had some military emails and credit card numbers (Mallone, 2016 and Barrett, 2016).

Whether or not the hacker actually has some military emails and credit card numbers has yet to be determined since he did not release the information and has not provided evidence to validate his statement (Barrett, 2016). Because this data breach was not as significant as the hack of the U.S. Office of Personnel Management, where the personal information of more than five million government employee were exposed, the Department of Homeland Security and the Department of Justice have downplayed the severity of the attack (Lee, 2016 and Barrett, 2016). Hopefully, the agencies learned an important lesson from this hack and found ways to improve their information security.

In order to improve their security, both agencies need to figure out how the attack occurred and create solutions that will help them avoid this problem in the future. According to reports, the hacker obtained the data after compromising a DOJ employee's email account; apparently the employee's password was sub-par (Storm, 2016). Because the DOJ employee's email account was not enough to access the DOJ web portal, the hacker contacted the appropriate department, social engineered his way in by telling the help desk he was new and did not know how to get past the portal, and ultimately gained access to the databases through the DOJ intranet once the attendant gave him the department's token code (Storm, 2016). By simply telling the attendant that he did not have a token code, the hacker was able to infiltrate the portal and have access to highly sensitive information (Storm, 2016 and Barrett, 2016).

After the hacker logged in and gained access, he clicked on a link to a personal computer; that took him to an online virtual machine where he entered in the credentials of the DOJ employee's email account—the one he already compromised (Storm, 2016). Once that was completed, the hacker was shown three different computers that he could access; one of them was the work computer of the DOJ employee that he originally hacked (Storm, 2016). The hacker then clicked on one of the computers and was fully admitted into it (Storm, 2016). Some of the privileges he had included access to both the user's documents and the other documents on the local network (Storm, 2016).

Although the data breach itself is problematic and the simplicity of the hack is not acceptable, the worst part about the whole situation is that it took the DOJ a week before it realized it had been breached—which the hacker tweeted about from the @DotGovs Twitter account (Storm, 2016).

Another embarrassment was that a reporter from Motherboard, who called Homeland Security's National Operations Center (NOC) to discuss the breached data, notified NOC of the leak; prior to that phone call, NOC was unaware of the incident (Storm, 2016).

Although this hack was an unfortunate situation, it was definitely eye-opening for both governmental agencies. Moving forward, it is safe to say that changes need to be made in order to improve information security at the Department of Homeland Security and the Department of Justice.

Statistics show that a lot of Americans—including government employees—fall prey to social engineering attacks. Solutions such as: verifying the identity of a person (on a call or via email) through authentication, having regular software updates, requiring employees to have strong passwords, creating patch policies, implementing a strong information security campaign that includes SETA (security, education, training, and awareness), enacting role-based security programs that are more personalized, determining which assets are valuable to cybercriminals in order to mitigate those risks, writing effective security policies that give employees some guidelines regarding how to handle specific situations, and enforcing those security policies help reduce the likelihood of an organization falling prey to an attack (Olavsrud, 2010).

Thankfully, most of the methods listed above are easily adoptable and inexpensive, so those solutions should at least be considered if not implemented. Reports indicate that proactive organizations that take information security seriously, utilize the tools listed above, and spend money on information security initiatives are seeing positive results—especially from a financial perspective; the more aware the employees are about information security, the less security breaches occur (SANS Institute InfoSec Reading Room, 2016).

As long as the Department of Homeland Security and the Department of Justice learned from their mistakes and have made changes that will reduce the likelihood of another social engineering attack or hack, I think that the incident served its purpose; it reminded both agencies of the importance of information security in the workplace and forced them to mitigate their risks more effectively.

References

Barrett, B. (2018, March 08). Hack Brief: Hacker Leaks the Info of Thousands of FBI and DHS Employees. Retrieved April 5, 2018, from https://www.wired.com/2016/02/hack-brief-fbi-and-dhs-are-targets-in-employee-info-hack/

Lee, D. (2016, February 09). 'Hack' on DoJ and DHS downplayed. Retrieved April 5, 2018, from https://www.bbc.com/news/technology-35529659

Mallonee, M. K. (2016, February 09). Hackers publish 20,000 FBI employees' contact information – CNNPolitics. Retrieved April 5, 2018, from https://www.cnn.com/2016/02/08/politics/hackers-fbi-employee-info/index.html

Olavsrud, T. (2010, October 19). 9 Best Defenses Against Social Engineering Attacks. Retrieved April 5, 2018, from https://www.esecurityplanet.com/views/article.php/390888 1/9-Best-Defenses-Against-Social-Engineering-Attacks.htm

SANS Institute InfoSec Reading Room. (2016, February). IT Security Spending Trends. Retrieved April 5, 2018, from https://www.sans.org/reading-room/whitepapers/analyst/security-spending-trends-36697

Storm, D. (2016, February 08). Hackers breach DOJ, dump details of 9,000 DHS employees, plan to leak 20,000 from FBI. Retrieved April 5, 2018, from https://www.computerworld.com/article/3030983/security/ hackers-breach-doj-dump-details-of-9-000-dhs-employees-plan-to-leak-20-000-from-fbi.html

4

MIRAI BOTNET IOT ATTACK

By: Charles Young

On the morning of October 21, 2016, as business was getting started on the East Coast of the United States; computer users noticed something odd. Many of their favorite websites were unreachable. It's not uncommon for a site to be occasionally offline, but multiple major sites offline concurrently is cause for concern. Internet heavyweights such as Amazon, Netflix, PayPal, Twitter, and many more were down (Maunder, 2016). It appeared to be a massive coordinated attack on multiple sites.

It was discovered that the cause of the massive outage was a Distributed Denial of Service (DDoS) attack on Dyn, an Infrastructure as a Service company which handles Domain Name Servers (DNS) and email (Dyn, n.d.). The attack didn't actually take down the sites or internet, but it did prohibit the proper functioning of the internet to the point that it appeared down to the average user.

This chapter will provide an in-depth study of the Dyn DNS attack, its impact on industry and the internet, and broader implications which arose as a result of the attack.

Much of the internet is facilitated through the use of the connection oriented protocol, Transmission Control Protocol (TCP) which utilizes a three-way handshake to establish connections between servers and clients. The three-way handshake occurs upon on initial contact between a client and server in order to establish a reliable connection prior to conducting business. The client will initiate the connection by sending a SYN (synchronize sequence numbers) packet to the server. The server will then respond with an ACK (acknowledgement) and SYN packet. The client will then send an ACK packet which will then complete the synchronization process and a reliable connection is established (Microsoft, n.d.).

The Dyn DNS attack used the TCP SYN flood attack which exploits the TCP three-way handshake. The attacker sends "repeated SYN packets to every port on the targeted server, often using a fake IP address" (Incapsula, n.d.). The targeted server dutifully attempts to establish communication by responding with a SYN-ACK packet from every open port. The attacker purposefully does not send the required ACK. Therefore, the targeted server will stand by waiting for the SYN-ACK packet. Before the connection is timed out, another SYN packet will arrive resulting in a half-open connection. With all open ports compromised, legitimate traffic is prevented access (Incapsula, n.d.).

Computers do not remember and read language as humans do. Therefore, to enable ease of use of the internet by both humans and computers, DNS was created. DNS takes human language internet addresses such as www.yahoo.com and converts it to the machine-readable internet protocol (IP) address 209.191.122.70. DNS servers can be local to the organization or outsourced to a managed DNS service, such as Dyn. The Dyn DNS attack specifically attacked port 53 on Dyn's servers. Port 53 is a well-known port, which is used by DNS and is commonly left open.

In conjunction with the TCP SYN flood attack, a prepend or subdomain attack was initiated. This attack "create[s] queries by prepending randomly generated subdomain strings to the victim's domain. E.g. xyz4433.yahoo.com" (Fulton, 2015). Not as many of these can be sent from each attacker, but they are harder to detect. The result of the subdomain attack is that the DNS server will flood queries for non-existent domains to the target domain, such as yahoo.com, from the aforementioned quote. The DNS server attempts to solicit or look up the nonexistent domain, thus preventing the server from handling legitimate requests.

The Dyn DNS attack occurred over three waves. The first wave attacked three Dyn datacenters in Chicago, Washington D.C. and New York (Greene, 2016). The second wave attacked 20 Dyn datacenters throughout the world. This was accomplished by having enough bots in each region to attack local Dyn DNS servers (Greene, 2016). The third wave was attempted but thwarted by Dyn's operations and support teams (York, 2016). Extensive planning and forethought was invested in order to ensure a successful attack across the world (Greene, 2016).

An attack of this scale could not be executed without the assistance of a botnet. Botnets are not new in computer attacks, but what is fascinating is the type of botnet utilized to execute the Dyn DNS attack.

The Dyn DNS attack utilized a relatively new botnet known as the Mirai botnet. It was first discovered during a "huge DDoS attack against the website of journalist Brian Krebs September 20, 2016" (Symantec, 2016). The Mirai botnet is unique in that it exploits the weak security of Internet of Things (IoT) devices. The IoT is the collective name of internet-connected home devices, such as smart TVs, CCTVs, and DVRs. Mirai continuously scans the internet for IoT devices with the intent to infect them exploiting their hardcoded user names and passwords (Symantec, 2016). It is estimated there are 50,000 to 100,000 IoT devices as part of the

Mirai botnet (Greene, 2016). Only about ten percent of the botnet was utilized for the Dyn DNS attack.

Dyn or any managed DNS provider was a smart choice by the attackers to create a massive outage while only focusing on attacking one organization. The masterminds designed the Dyn DNS attack to have far-reaching, global impact.

The Dyn DNS attack had technological and financial repercussions. During the attack, the botnet traffic created massive congestion which cut off "legitimate traffic not even headed for Dyn" (Greene, 2016). Some major internet backbone providers had to reroute traffic to avoid congestion (Greene, 2016). Additionally, Dyn customers had either backup DNS providers to which they switched to during the attack or found an alternative to avoid the outage. A Chinese electronics firm that manufactured many of the compromised webcams, issued an immediate recall (Symantec, 2016).

The loss of business during the outage was not quantified, however, given the sheer number of organizations affected, significant profit loss is a certainty. Some of the businesses affected were financial services companies, too. Dyn was not immune to the fallout from the attack. Estimates are roughly 8% of Dyn's customer base stopped using their services in the aftermath of the attack (Weagle, 2017).

Perhaps the most problematic issue with the Dyn DNS attack is the botnet. The Mirai botnet was relatively new and had only been observed briefly prior to the attack on Dyn. However, the actual attack perpetrated by the Mirai botnet was a SYN flood attack which is quite well-known and can be mitigated through many well tested strategies. The Dyn DNS engineers worked tirelessly to stop the attack on the organization and put out precautionary measures to prevent future incidents.

Even though Dyn did an outstanding job stopping the attack and getting DNS servers back online, the botnet was left untouched. Additionally, there does not seem to be adequate interest in thwarting the botnet from IoT device manufactures. Specifically, many of the "… insecure IoT or internet-connected devices are no longer in line for security updates, which makes it possible for hackers to hijack these connected devices today or tomorrow" (Khandelwal, 2016).

The Dyn DNS attack will be remembered for the conscription of IoT devices into a botnet to carry out a DDoS attack. This may also mark the beginning of a disturbing trend in using IoT devices to carry out attacks. IoT manufactures should be aware of this possibility and proper security precautions should be taken to harden IoT devices. Additionally, organizations should take this incident as a cautionary tale regarding DNS management and emergency situations. DNS management should be part of an organization's continuity of operations plan.

References

Microsoft. (n.d.) Explanation of the Three-Way Handshake via
TCP/IP. Retrieved August 19, 2017, from
https://support.microsoft.com/en-
us/help/172983/explanation-of-the-three-way-handshake-
via-tcp-ip

Fulton, S. (2015, February 20). Top 10 DNS attacks likely to
infiltrate your network. Retrieved
August 19, 2017, from
http://www.networkworld.com/article/2886283/security0/to
p-10- dns-attacks-likely-to-infiltrate-your-network.html

Greene, T. (2016, October 21). How the Dyn DDoS attack
unfolded. Retrieved August 19, 2017, from
http://www.networkworld.com/article/3134057/security/ho
w-the-dyn-ddos-attack-unfolded.html

Khandelwal, S. (2016, September 27). World's largest 1 Tbps DDoS
Attack launched from 152,000 hacked Smart Devices.
Retrieved August 20, 2017, from
http://thehackernews.com/2016/09/ddos-attack-iot.html

Maunder, M. (2016, October 21). DynDNS is currently being

DDoS'd - May affect your site. Retrieved August 17, 2017, from https://www.wordfence.com/blog/2016/10/dyndns-currently-ddosd-may-affect-site/

Symantec. (n.d.). Mirai: what you need to know about the botnet behind recent major DDoS attacks. Retrieved August 19, 2017, from ttp://www.symantec.com/connect/blogs/mirai-what-you-need-know-about-botnet-behind-recent-major-ddos-attacks

Incapsula. (n.d.). What is a TCP SYN Flood | DDoS Attack Glossary | Retrieved August 19, 2017, from https://www.incapsula.com/ddos/attack-glossary/syn-flood.html

Dyn. (n.d.). Working With Us. Retrieved August 17, 2017, from https://dyn.com/working-with-us/

York, K. (2016, October 22). Dyn Statement on 10/21/2016 DDoS Attack | Dyn Blog. Retrieved August 19, 2017, from https://dyn.com/blog/dyn-statement-on-10212016-ddos-attack/

5

VERIZON

By: Austin Ludwig

In early March of 2016, Verizon Enterprise Solutions was attacked. Verizon Enterprise Solutions, a division of Verizon Communications, is a large telecommunications company that specializes in helping some of the largest companies in the world respond to their own data breaches. About ninety-nine percent of Fortune 500 companies are using Verizon Enterprise Solutions (KrebsOnSecurity, 2016).

A prominent member of a closely guarded underground cybercrime forum posted a new thread advertising the sale of a database containing the contact information of around one million and a half Verizon Enterprise customers. Verizon Enterprises discovered and patched the security vulnerability on their enterprise client portal, but not before the vulnerability could be compromised (KrebsOnSecurity, 2016).

It is believed that the most probable cause of the breach was a SQL injection vulnerability. Verizon Enterprises uses an online database platform called MongoDB. MongoDB databases are not subject to traditional sql injection attacks. However, MongoDB databases are still subject to new injection attacks, which can be leveraged to extract data from the MongoDB (Barth, 2016).

Tens of thousands of organizations use MongoDB to store data. Unfortunately, misconfiguring and leaving the database exposed online can be easy. For example, if the default settings are left intact, MongoDB allows anyone to browse the database, download them, or even write over and delete them. Since Verizon's database was left publicly accessible, obtaining customer information was relatively easy (KrebsOnSecurity, 2017).

Once the cybercriminal obtained the stolen data, this information was posted on the underground cybercrime forum. This information, which contained approximately 1.5 million customer contact information records could be bought in sections. 100,000 records could be purchased for ten thousand dollars apiece. Along with the stolen data, buyers were also offered the option to purchase information regarding security vulnerabilities in Verizon's website (KrebsOnSecurity, 2016).

The fact that Verizon Enterprise Solutions is a high-profile security vendor makes this very embarrassing. Even with a good security program in place, any organization is never immune to attacks. It only takes one mistake to create an opportunity for an attacker to exploit (McGee, 2016). Any successful attack on an organization can produce negative effects, but an attack of this magnitude can significantly damage their reputation. Current customers and potential customers may begin to question or reconsider using Verizon in the future which can greatly hurt revenue.

Even though only basic contact information was stolen, cybercriminals can use this information to target these customers using phishing or other targeted attacks. Cybercriminals can pose as an employee in the IT department or any other trusted employee to gain confidential information which could become quite damaging. Employees are often said to be the weakest link regarding security so extra precaution is needed to help combat these attacks.

If potential breaches are to be prevented in the future, Verizon must discover and respond to vulnerabilities more efficiently and strive to reduce breaches. This can be achieved by using vulnerability assessments which provide numerous security benefits. The Center for Internet Security lists continuous vulnerability assessments and remediation as one of the first five controls that can help reduce security risks. These assessments can be used to target remediation plans, as well as highlight systemic issues, including gaps in patch management or asset life cycle management (ISACA, 2017).

In addition to vulnerability assessments, having an appropriate incident response plan in place can be vital. These days, it is becoming a reality of when an organization will be attacked and not if an attack will occur. Tabletop exercises and drills can prove to be vital because the attack may not always be what people remember most, but rather how the organization responds to the attack (McGee, 2016).

As a result of the Verizon Enterprise Solutions attack, there are lessons to be learned. One lesson is that being attacked or successfully attacked is becoming more common. With successful attacks becoming commonplace, it is of upmost importance to continuously test for flaws and any possible vulnerabilities in the security. Unfortunately, many organizations may not think of testing as important as it should be due to difficulty determining potential losses from a breach.

Although organizations may not feel the need to take preventative measures if there has not been a breach in the past, benefits can be reaped in the future. Preventative measures may seem like a waste of time and money, but the cost to react to a breach can cost much more money, along with the potential damage to their reputation. When critical errors are found before they can become a problem, it justifies testing early and often. There is a possibility that Verizon could have prevented this breach with early testing.

In March of 2016, Verizon Enterprise Solutions was found to have been a victim of a data breach. The vulnerability was quickly patched, but not before a prominent member of an underground cybercrime forum posted contact information of around one million and a half Verizon Enterprise customers. In addition, the cybercriminal posted vulnerabilities discovered in Verizon's website. This breach was particularly embarrassing as Verizon Enterprises helps some of the largest companies in the world respond to data breaches of their own. To avoid or mitigate breaches in the future, it is imperative to conduct vulnerability assessments along with preparing an incident response plan. Also, testing early and often is vital. With these measures in place, security can be greatly hardened to help prevent and mitigate potential attacks in the future.

References

Barth, B. (2016, March 25). Data breach authority Verizon
    Enterprise breached; 1.5 millioncustomers impacted.
    Retrieved from https://www.scmagazine.com/data-breach-

authorityverizon-enterprise-breached-15-million-customers-impacted/article/528663/

ISACA. (n.d.). VULNERABILITY ASSESSMENT. Retrieved 2017, from https://cybersecurity.isaca.org/info/cyberaware/images/ISACA_WP_Vulnerability_Assessment_1117.pdf

ITRC. (n.d.). Data Breaches Increase 40 Percent in 2016, Finds New Report from Identity TheftResource Center and CyberScout. Retrieved from https://www.idtheftcenter.org/2016databreaches.html

Krebs, B. (2016, March 24). Krebs on Security. Retrieved from https://krebsonsecurity.com/2016/03/crooks-steal-sell-verizon-enterprise-customer-data/

Krebs, B. (2017, January 10). Krebs on Security. Retrieved from https://krebsonsecurity.com/tag/mongodb/

McGee, M. K. (2016, March 25). Verizon Confirms Breach Affecting Business Customers. Retrieved from https://www.bankinfosecurity.com/verizon-confirms-breach-affectingbusiness-customers-a-8991

6

MEDSTAR HEALTH

By: Jonathan Lancelot

Health emergencies can happen to anyone at any time in their lives. Hospitals are set up to provide emergency and extensive care for those in need, and in the 21st-century, computer networks and technology give hospitals the capability to care for millions. In 2016, this was called into question when ten hospitals computer networks were hit with a ransomware attack, locking up the system healthcare professionals and patients depend upon. "Ransomware is a strain of malware that encrypts data on infected machines, then typically asks users to pay ransom in hard-to-trace digital currency to get an electronic key so they can retrieve their data" (Williams). The disruption of service was significant enough that patients were turned away or treated without access to historical patient records. "Some patients said their appointments had been canceled or rescheduled because doctors could not access medical records in the first few days of the computer attack" (Williams), which would have been devastating for patients who have complicated health conditions that require a study patient history, or a patient with allergies to specific medicine that requires immediate treatment.

Given the health risks posed by a ransomware cyber-attack on a hospital's computer network, the exposure of patient confidential information can lead to legal and reputational risk. Most of all, the threat to patient privacy can be a significant concern if healthcare administrators do not undertake risk management strategies. "The attack on MedStar Health forced the hospital chain, which served hundreds of thousands of patients, to shut down its email and health records database in an effort to keep the virus from spreading further throughout the organization. The incident follows similar cyber-attacks targeting at least three other medical institutions in recent weeks" (Pennic). Given a hospital's computer network is an essential component of its service infrastructure, shutting down the system used as a preventative control or countermeasure in response to a cyber-attack could spell disaster for safety and continuous operations.

Within the year itself, a number of cyber-attacks on other hospital computer networks can be perceived as a full-scale assault. "Ransomware was on the rise with attacks on Chino Valley Medical Center and its sister site Desert Valley Medical

Center in California, and Methodist Hospital in Kentucky within the month. Shortly before those, Hollywood Presbyterian was forced to pay cybercriminals $17, 000 in Bitcoin in mid-February" (Monegain). It is not difficult to see that hospitals were under pressure to either hold out on ransom payment and endanger the lives of patients or pay and continue regular operations. In fact, "the Federal Bureau of Investigations (FBI) urged victims not to pay the ransom –advice many find hard to follow" (Williams), and who can blame hospital administrators for wanting to pay. While no one wants cybercriminals to get away with extortion, take a hospital hostage, and outright fraud, the risk of compromising the health of patients is too high to ignore. This vice is the target of these cyber operations.

We can deduce that the lack of preparedness opened Medstar to the ransomware cyber-attack that in-turn led to the compromising position of choosing to pay the ransom or endanger the lives of patients by halting operations completely to flush the worm out of the system. "Cyber-attack and data breach prevention strategies should be considered an integral part of daily business operations at hospitals. Ultimately, no defense is impregnable against determined adversaries" (Fuentes, Huq, page. 38), yet it is better than not being prepared for the unexpected. A hospital computer network system has to be prepared for other types of cyber-attacks, not just ransomware as in this case. First, "firmware attacks are where perpetrators can access and modify the firmware source code of a medical device to add backdoors, which can then be pushed out via existing auto-update mechanisms" (Fuentes, Huq, page.28). Second, "there are more than 250, 000 mHealth apps for mobile devices. mHealth mobile apps can be compromised to change functionality, deliver fatal-level dosage, expose personal health data, penetrate other company systems, and cause Health Insurance Portability and Accountability Act (HIPAA violations" (Fuentes, Huq, page. 28). Third, "perpetrators can access and modify the source code of a vendor by installing a backdoor or rooting the device. Because hospitals tend not to test device security before installing it on their networks, this can cause malware infections, exfiltration of data, and sharing data with third-party vendors or advertisers" (Fuentes, Huq, page. 29). Fourth, insider threats can be intentional, for example, data theft, or unintentional, for example, accidental disclosure or disposal of records" (Fuentes, Huq, page. 29). Fifth, "perpetrators can attempt to compromise hospital websites, Electronic Health Records (EHR) software, and internal portals used by hospital staff and vendors" (Fuentes, Huq, page. 30). Lastly, through the tactic of "spear phishing from trusted email accounts, perpetrators can gain control of vendor credentials and send clients emails that appear legitimate" (Fuentes, Huq, page. 30). In the case of Medstar, ransomware was the documented method of attack employed against hospital networks, yet any of the other methods of attack enumerated could be implemented with stealth and without detection if successful.

Despite the reports of the possibility of a catastrophic cyber-attack on their computer network, officials at Medstar defended their preparedness strategy post-event. "MedStar said, 90 percent of its systems were back up and running, and close-to-normal number of patients had passed through the doors of its facilities during the outages" (Duncan, McDaniels). MedStar also stated they "opened command centers to deal with the crisis, and information technology teams worked to identify the malware and moved to block it" (Duncan, McDaniels). MedStar did not pay the ransom according to the same authority. Additionally, MedStar took a defensive stance stating that "the media coverage featuring criminal acts –offenses against the public that are punishable –perpetuates the infamy of malicious attacks for airtime and publicity" (Duncan, McDaniel). In other words, the situation was blown out of proportion by reports of the cyber-attack. Nevertheless, overblown or not, Cris Thomas from Tenable Network Security states "healthcare, in general, has not had a very good track record with information security" (Duncan, McDaniel), and has "conducted a survey of several industries, and ranked healthcare companies' computer security as below average" (Duncan, McDaniels). Consequently, these companies run the risk of reputational damage from being reactive instead of preemptive in their approach to cybersecurity.

The control measure undertook by MedStar by shutting down the system to fix it is controversial at best. When MedStar discovered what it called a virus within its critical systems, it was too late to take those steps. Instead, the company's response was to pull everything offline" (Duncan, McDaniels). This maneuver can make any attempt to investigate by forensics difficult, yet aside from this, most cybersecurity professionals would advise against it. "A security analyst who spoke to The Sun have questioned the move which they called an extreme measure that harked back to the responses of the 1990s. The move can be seen as a panic mode, and even though disconnecting and unplugging sort of works, it is not a viable solution today" (Duncan, McDaniels). MedStar defended itself by "calling the decision courageous and mission-critical. The health system said law enforcement and cybersecurity experts praised the move as a critical component in the resulting recovery time" (Duncan, McDaniels). For a hospital or any high-reliability organization, recovery time is crucial.

Conversely, from a cybersecurity perspective, preemptive control measures are the other crucial halves of the equation that were missing. "Preventative controls are the road barriers of the information highway. They are designed to stop an attacker from getting to an asset. If the asset involves physical protection, then a good example of a prevention control would be security guards. Digital equivalents of the security guard include antivirus and antimalware applications, cybersecurity awareness training, data loss prevention, firewalls, gateways, and intrusion prevention systems" (Moschovitis, page. 131-133). Without these security measures in place, an organization will be in a continuous state of reaction instead of a state of risk management.

Risk Management is an endeavor that is a continuous operation for an organization, "an ongoing process of identifying, assessing, and responding to risk. To manage the risk of a cyber-attack, organizations ought to assess the likelihood and potential impact of an event and then determine the best approach to deal with the risks: avoid, transfer, accept, or mitigate" (Tobar). As it is not known if MedStar had a risk management plan in place, given the gravitas of the ransomware cyber-attack on hospital computer networks, and the reaction of the company to the presence of the bug, proper detective controls were missing that could have alerted the system before it metastasized into a full-blown system shutdown. "detective controls are the motion detection sensors that let you know that someone is in the room. The idea behind them is to detect abnormalities and raise the alarm" (Moschovitis, page.133). Even with all the preparation, sometimes nerves can cause bad decisions to be made, and this is why employee training is critical to any incident-response planning.

How did the ransomware get into the hospital's computer networking system in the first place? Through software vulnerabilities within exploitable hardware components. "The ransomware attack occurred after hackers discovered that MedStar Health uses JBoss, an application server with a recognized design flaw. The hackers used Samas, or 'samsam,' a virus-like software, to scan the internet for vulnerable JBoss Servers" (LaPointe). The externality from this attack could have been mitigated if MedStar with have heeded the warning from "security researchers found that the JBoss application server was 'routinely misconfigured to allow unauthorized outside users to gain control" (LaPointe). In other words, there was no move by Medstar manage the risk as "they could have fixed the vulnerability by installing a patch for the system or manually deleting two lines of software code" (LaPointe). The company again defended itself by stating they "maintain constant surveillance of its IT networks in concert with our outsider IT partners and cybersecurity experts" (LaPointe), yet in reality hospital data was compromised. As a result, the ransomware entered the JBoss Servers and seized critical systems. Next, "Medstar employees encountered a pop-up message demanding payment of 45 bitcoin, approximately $19,000 in exchange for a digital key that would unlock the data, according to several reports. The malware has blocked MedStar employees from accessing patient data and, in some cases, having to turn patients away" (McCarthy). The company had ample forewarning as "the US government, Red Hat Inc., and other groups released warnings about the security issue in February 2007 and March 2010. The warnings explicitly stated that the security problem could allow unauthorized users to access confidential information and potentially disrupt business operations" (LaPointe). MedStar failed to act and manage the risk, and defended its actions in the aftermath despite signs of failure.

An organization without an incidence-response plan is like a fighter jet flying at night without an instrument flight reference system, as soon as the aircraft is angling into a mountain endangering the life of the pilot, the pilot is not aware of the danger as he believes he is still flying level and above any terrestrial surfaces. When disaster strikes, it's too late to react. "The core phase of incident-response planning is preparing for incidents, identifying the occurrence of an incident, containing the incident, treating the incident, recovering from the incident, and post-incident review, aka the lessons-learned phase. The last one is key and should never be omitted" (Moschovitis, page. 150). Anything short of being prepared for the worst is demonstrating a lack of foresight and leadership needed in an age where computer networks are the nerve centers of organizational operations.

In an ideal world, hospitals would be off limits to any catastrophic attack, whether it physical or cyber, yet we know that is not the case. Regarding the former, "it is undeniable that despite the Geneva Conventions, hospitals have been attacked in many conflicts. But the pattern, frequency, and nature of these attacks have changed considerably over the last few years. Recently termed the 'weaponization' of health care, bombing hospitals has become part of a multi-dimensional war strategy which uses large scale violence to systematically and deliberately target medical facilities, depriving people of their access to healthcare" (Thomas). Given that this chapter is focused on cyber-attacks on hospital computer systems, the same principle applies. There is no reason to attack a hospital's critical system as it is a place where the most vulnerable and sick get care from healthcare professional use technology to save the lives of their patient, other than the reason to inflict harm for the sake of taking the advantage. This can fall into the realm of cyber-warfare, which would fit our situation above that address's physical attacks on hospitals. In other words, cyberspace is a virtual and lawless territory where anarchy is the norm, and cyber operations with the intent to commit a crime will do so without regard to the lives that will be affected. With this reality in mind, companies that are responsible for safeguarding the technology on which hospitals depends upon must be vigilant in avoiding a comparable situation to the MedStar incident.

References

Duncan, I., & McDaniels, A. K. (2016, April 2). MedStar hack shows risks that come with electronic heath records. *Baltimore Sun*. Retrieved from www.baltimoresun.com/health/bs-md.medstar-healthcare-hack-20160402-story-html

Fuentes, M. R., & Huq, N. (2018). Securing Connected Hospitals: A Research on Exposed Medical Systems and Supply Chain Risks. *TrendLabs: Trend Micro,*1-60.

LaPointe, J. (2016, April 7). MedStar Ransomware Attack Caused by Known Security Flaw. *Health IT Security*. Retrieved February 27, 2019, from healthitsecurity.com/news/medstar-ransomware-attack-caused-by-known-security-flaw

Monegain, B. (2016, March 29). MedStar Health hacked, computer virus locks out employees at Georgetown University Hospital. *Healthcare Finance News*.

Moschovitis, C. (n.d.). *Cybersecurity Program Development for Business: The Essential Planning Guide*. Hoboken, NJ: Wiley.

Pennic, F. (2016, March 30). MedStar Cyber Attack Shows Need for HHS to Implement Cybersecurity Law. *HIT Consultant Media*.

Thomas, K. (2018, November 27). Stop Bombing Hospitals: Why the World Needs the. Retrieved from www.epijournal.com/home/2018/11/27/a-new-paradigm-of-war-the-weaponization-of-heathcare

Tobar, D. (2018, February 9). 7 Considerations for Cyber Risk Management. Retrieved from insights.sei.cmu.edu/insider-threat/2018/02/7-considerations-for-cyber-risk-management.html

Carnegie Mellon University: Software Engineering Institute

Williams, P. (2016, March 31). Medstar Hospitals Recovering After 'Ransomware' Hack. *NBC News.*

7

WENDY'S

By: Jeff Falcon

In January 2016, a nationwide investigation of credit card fraud was launched by several banking and financial institutions into the criminal theft and loss of personal credit card information handled by Wendy's. This would later become public knowledge beginning in May 2016.

Wendy's network of systems spans across approximately 5,500 franchise and company-operated restaurants in the United States and 28 countries and U.S. territories worldwide (Krebs, 2016). A company released statement at the time, outlined the investigation.

> "Based on the preliminary findings of the investigation and other information, the Company believes that malware, installed through the use of compromised third-party vendor credentials, affected one particular point of sale systems at fewer than 300 of approximately 5,500

franchised North America Wendy's restaurants, starting in the fall of 2015."

In an open letter to consumers published by Wendy's President and CEO Todd Penegor on July 7, 2016, discussed the further discovery of additional malicious cyber activity resulting from compromised credentials. This compromise resulted in the ability for the criminal adversaries to remotely deploy malware on some of the franchisees' point-of-sale systems giving indication that the original reported outbreak was larger than originally reported by Wendy's (Wendy's, 2016). The growing complexity, sophistication and evasive cybercriminal tactics which complicate and prolong cyber investigations further reinforce the pervasiveness and overall reach of a cyberattack. Wendy's confirmed that cybercriminals compromised and stole customer data including cardholder names, debit and credit card numbers and expiration dates.

Abbreviated Timeline of Events

- Late Fall 2015: Wendy's breached with malware on point-of-sale (POS) systems.
- January 2016: Wendy's acknowledges a potential investigation to a breach as reported by journalist Brian Krebs (Krebs, 2016).
- February 2016: Wendy's confirms that cybersecurity experts discovered malware in a small subset of locations but

further estimates of the outbreak could not be estimated (Wendy's Financial Results, 2016).

- April 2016: Financial Institutions continue to report indications of the breach still compromising customer cardholder information (Krebs, 2016).
- June 2016: Wendy's revises their statement announcing "the number of franchise restaurants impacted by these cybersecurity attacks is now expected to be considerably higher than the 300 restaurants already impacted" (Wendy's Financial Results, 2016).
- July 2016: Wendy's released updated list of locations impacted by the breach to 1,025 total locations. (Wendy's Update, 2016)

What is significant about this attack is the attack vector was through a third party "service provider" that had remote access to the point of sale terminals and cash registers (Krebs, 2017). Similar to the attacks on Target and Home Depot in 2014, third part vendors pose a significant risk to retailers. It is important to require any third party that has access to corporate networks to meet the same security posture as the parent organization.

Given the lengthy timelines of the Wendy's data breach, it is obvious that great improvements are needed to help build and sustain an organization's resilience in the moment and after a cyberattack. This will require a vigilant and continuous effort in order to close the margin on cyber criminals. Organizations need to embed security into their culture and overall fabric of their organization to improve their ability to prevent, detect and react under pressure.

Digital Transformation in Security

Innovative new business models, executive endorsement and a strong risk-based governance program, are critical components helping forge the modernization, evolution and maturity of security programs. Breakthrough technologies that assist with monitoring of anomalous and suspicious activity, improvements within automation and orchestration of response procedures and the incorporation of tactical threat intelligence, are emerging and being adopted in the market. Additionally, the evolution and recent importance placed upon endpoint system security has paved the way to allow the entry of Artificial Intelligence and Machine Learning to enter the conversation. AI/ML technologies offer another approach to help defend against a growing arsenal of highly sophisticated tools and techniques commonly used to exploit and compromise critical digital assets. According to Joe Levy, Chief Technology Officer of IT Security Company Sophos, "The biggest strength of ML is making predictions more efficiently than humans". This translates into a faster, more efficient and highly scalable solution at much lower

2016 Annual Report of Top Cyber Security Incidents

error rates than conventional prevention and detection
technologies. Levy also states,

> "ML gives us a greater ability than ever to identity
> malware that we don't know about, and which we didn't
> even have an idea existed". In practical terms, that often
> means threats that use new evasion techniques designed
> to avoid detection. These are often the entry points for
> backdoors, data harvesting trojans, credential harvesting
> tools and other techniques used in larger attacks" (Levy,
> 2018).

Although no single silver bullet solution exists, ML by itself
and for that matter pure malware detection simply isn't enough.
A component of an intelligent, orchestrated layered protection
strategy, technologies such as ML will greatly increase the ability
for an organization to find the needle in the haystack, improving
response time and recovery from a cyberattack (Sophos, 2018).

References

Krebs, Brian. Krebs on Security. Wendy's Probes Reports of
    Credit Card Breach. January 27, 2016
    https://krebsonsecurity.com/2016/01/wendys-probes-
    reports-of-credit-card-breach/
Wendy's Payment Card Incident Statement. Statement of

Todd Penegor President and CEO, The Wendy's Company.
July 7, 2016
https://www.wendys.com/payment-card-incident

Wendy's Update, PR Newswire. Wendy's Update on Unusual
Credit Card Activity. June 9, 2016.
http://ir.wendys.com/phoenix.zhtml?c=67548&p=irol-newsArticle&ID=2176721

Wendy's Financial Release. February 9, 2016.
http://ir.wendys.com/phoenix.zhtml?c=67548&p=irol-newsArticle&ID=2136634

Sophos, Naked Security. 2018.
https://nakedsecurity.sophos.com/

Levy, Joe. Chief Technology Officer, Sophos. Personal
Communication. 2018.
https://www.sophos.com/en-us/company/management/joe-levy.aspx

8

ADULT FRIEND FINDER

By: Lyda Tesauro

According to Leaked Source, a data breach monitoring service, Adult Friend Finder was hacked again in less than two years; this time, though, the hack was one of the biggest data breaches ever reported in 2016 (Storm, 2016). Currently, the 2014 Yahoo attack is the only exploit that has more accounts compromised (Peterson, 2016; Ragan, 2016). With over six databases jeopardized and more than 412 million hacked accounts linked to AdultFriendFinder.com, Cams.com, iCams.com, Stripshow.com, Penthouse.com, and an unknown domain, Adult Friend Finder definitely gained some notoriety in the press (Ragan, 2016). Considering the nature of the website and the service it provides, Adult Friend Finder should have made more of an effort to secure their networks. Maybe then, the organization could have avoided millions of users having their personal information stolen, published, and sold on online criminal marketplaces (Gibbs, 2016; Ragan, 2016).

Because the California based company is an X-rated adult dating and entertainment organization, Adult Friend Finder members past and present were probably mortified that their sexual secrets were accessible and exposed (Whittaker, 2016). Generally speaking, no one involved in deviant sexual behavior would want those practices made public. Instead, members of sites like Adult Friend Finder would rather have that side of their life kept secret so that they can avoid judgement from society and exploitation from cybercriminals. Some individuals who definitely did not want their names and personal information associated with Adult Friend Finder were the 5,650 people who used .gov email addresses and the 78,301 people who used .mil email addresses to register their accounts (Cluley, 2016; Gibbs, 2016). By involving themselves in the Adult Friend Finder community and trusting a company that did not have effective information security measures in place, the victims of the breach opened themselves up to blackmail, extortion, phishing attacks, and other cyber fraud scams (Gibbs, 2016; Lima, 2016). If Adult Friend Finder had put information security at the forefront of their firm, they probably would not have had to answer for their system's technological flaws or had to face the legal ramifications that accompany a data breach.

From a technological standpoint, Adult Friend Finder and Friend Finder Networks (FFN) should have mitigated their risks more effectively. Prior to the incident, a security researcher whose alias is Revolver or 1x0123 on Twitter warned Adult Friend Finder in October about the local file inclusion (LFI) vulnerabilities on their website and posted screenshots to justify the claim (Whittaker, AdultFriendFinder network hack exposes 412 million accounts, 2016). Revolver notified the company of the vulnerability because if it was discovered in the module on Adult Friend Finder's production servers and was successfully exploited, it could have allowed an attacker to remotely run malicious code on the web server (Whittaker, 2016). Although Revolver claimed that the issue was resolved and "no customer information ever left the site," the security researcher was unfortunately wrong (Ragan, 2016). A couple days later, Steve Ragan of CSO's Salted Hash reported that Friend Finder Networks "had likely been compromised despite Revolver's claims, exposing more than 100 million accounts" (Ragan, 2016; Storm, 2016). The early estimates of that report indicated that public and private key pairs had been leaked; it also mentioned that the existence of source code from Friend Finder Networks' production environment had been discovered (Ragan, 2016). Amidst those findings, multiple entities additionally claimed that they had access to AdultFriendFinder.com records (Ragan, 2016). With all the evidence collected, it became clear that Adult Friend Finder and Friend Finder Networks had suffered "a severe data breach" (Ragan, 2016).

Naturally, the organization that boasts the "world's largest sex and swinger community" initially followed typical big-business protocol where they neither confirmed nor denied the attack that happened in October; however, the adult-oriented flagship company, Friend Finder Networks, eventually informed the public in November that they did find a vulnerability and, at that time, were working to fix it (Whittaker, 2016). According to Whittaker, the latest results regarding the hack in November indicated that six FFN databases were breached and that users of an underground Russian hacking site (a claim made by Revolver) could have been responsible for the cyber incident (Whittaker, 2016). Reports revealed that the compromised data consisted of about 20 years' worth of e-mail addresses (mostly Hotmail, Yahoo, and Gmail accounts), passwords (that were stored either in plaintext or hashed using SHA1 with pepper), membership statuses (i.e. whether or not the member was a VIP), browser information, purchases made, login information (i.e. the IP address last used to login), and over 15 million deleted accounts (Whittaker, 2016; Cluley, 2016). Due to the nature of the breach and the information it contained, Leaked Source decided to break with tradition and not make the data searchable; however, that did not mean that Adult Friend Finder users' information was inaccessible to cybercriminals or hackers (Whittaker, 2016). In order to better understand the logistics of the cyber incident, a breakdown of the exposed databases and unacceptable password practices is shown below (Storm, 2016).

Password	Frequency
123456	900,420
12345	635,995
123456789	585,150
12345678	145,867
1234567890	133,414
1234567	112,956
password	101,046
qwerty	86,050
qwertyuiop	43,755
987654321	40,627

Table 1. Top AFF passwords (Storm, 2016)

As shown in table 1, a vast number of passwords were either in plaintext or hashed using SHA1 pepper (Storm, 2016). According to experts, neither method Adult Friend Finder or the mothership, Friend Finder Networks, used to secure passwords is considered an acceptable practice (Storm, 2016). To make matters worse, the hashed passwords appeared to have been changed to all lowercase before storage; this makes them far easier to attack, but also means the credentials will be slightly less useful for threat agents to abuse (Ragan, 2016). Although Adult Friend Finder is mostly to blame for this incident, some of the end users definitely needed to have had better passwords—especially if they were engaging in that kind of activity. Because of the company's poor security practices and the users' ridiculous password creations, Leaked Source was able to crack 99% of the passwords—even passwords that were 32 characters in length (Storm, 2016). Examples of the types of passwords used can be found below (Storm, 2016).

If Adult Friend Finder users or other users that engage in scandalous activities do not want to be exposed and have their passwords cracked, they need to create strong passwords, never re-use them, and change them somewhat frequently (Cluley, 2016). According to information security experts around the world, passwords containing simple number or letter sequences, personal information, meaningful words, and predictable areas of interest are not safe to use (Riley, 2006). Passwords that utilize acronyms or contain uppercase letters, lowercase letters, numbers, and special characters are definitely more secure. Other ways users can protect themselves from being both hacked and blackmailed are: they can abstain from sites like Adult Friend Finder, they can utilize burner email accounts to avoid immediate exposure (only if refraining is not an option), and they can delete accounts that are linked to inappropriate sites—although deletion does not guarantee the account's details will actually be erased (Cluley, 2016). Lastly, frequent users of sites like Adult Friend Finder need to educate themselves on cybersecurity issues and practices in order to help mitigate their risk of being exploited; however, that is not enough to curb data breaches. Corporations also need to take information security more seriously and they need to secure their networks more effectively.

One way Friend Finder Networks (including Adult Friend Finder) could have eliminated their local file inclusion vulnerability was to avoid passing user submitted input to any filesystem/framework API (OWASP, 2015). If that was not a viable option, the company also could have maintained a white list of files (that could be included by the page) and then used an identifier (e.g. the index number) to access the selected file (OWASP, 2015). Furthermore, in order to avoid having an LFI vulnerability in the future, the organization needs to always reject any request containing an invalid identifier—this will ensure that there will never be an attack surface for malicious users to manipulate the path (OWASP, 2015). Hopefully, both organizations are aware of these remedies and will enact these practices so that, in the future, the companies' will never face another hack due to a LFI vulnerability.

Typically, with scandalous sites like these, customers expect companies to protect their data, diligently find as well as fix vulnerabilities as soon as possible, and ensure that their secrets never reach the mainstream media. When users do not receive what a company is supposed to provide and are exposed, affected individuals usually invoke legal action. Since this is the second time hackers have infiltrated Friend Finder networks—compromising about 4 million accounts in 2015—and serious changes were not made to mitigate their risk, Adult Friend Finder and Friend Finder Networks will eventually have to pay millions of dollars in damages as a settlement to a class-action lawsuit; they will also have to worry about finding the funds to pay for those damages since the firm declared bankruptcy in 2013, and they will have to do some serious damage control to repair their reputation (Lima, 2016). Because of the scale of the breach and the gross negligence on their part, Adult Friend Finder will have a hard time overcoming this cyber incident—especially with the looming threat of potential regulatory action by governmental agencies, potential involvement of the state consumer protection bureau, and potential intervention from the FTC (Lima, 2016).

Even though Adult Friend Finder did not intentionally jeopardize their members' account information, the company will probably not receive any leniency from the FTC due to the precedence the FTC set in the 2015 case against international hotel and resort chain, Wyndham Hotels (Lima, 2016). In the 2015 suit, the FTC claimed that the company had enough warning to properly mitigate the problem, but instead did not take the necessary steps to prevent it; therefore, the case constituted an unfair business practice (Lima, 2016). Because Adult Friend Finder waited a week before admitting publicly that their networks were compromised, did not modernize and patch vulnerabilities after their first breach, fell prey to the same vulnerability that allowed them to be hacked in 2015, and did not force users to reset their passwords when they logged in next (a standard practice after a data breach), the organization will likely not receive any sympathy from the public or the appropriate governing bodies (Lima, 2016) (Whittaker, 2016). The organization's ineffective communication with customers, the lack of proactiveness, and the firm's downplay of the breach (see the official statement below) decreased the firm's chance at redemption and only infuriated Adult Friend Finder members more (Whittaker, 2016). Hopefully, in the future, Adult Friend Finder will be more forthcoming with information if they fall prey to another security breach and will give more guidance to their customers throughout the whole ordeal.

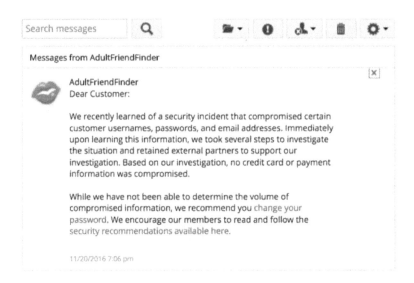

Figure 1. (Whittaker, 2016).

Although Adult Friend Finder probably wishes this incident never happened to them, the company did learn very important lessons that will help them avoid other security breaches in the future. The organization learned the hard way that accepting certain risks without just cause will hurt them in the long-run. According to Whitman and Mattord, a firm only has just cause to "accept" or "do nothing to protect a vulnerability" once the organization has "determined the level of risk posed to the information asset, assessed the probability of attack and the likelihood of a successful exploitation of a vulnerability, estimated the potential damage or loss that could result from attacks, evaluated potential controls using each appropriate type of feasibility, performed a thorough risk assessment (including a financial analysis such as a CBA), and decided that the costs to control the risk to a particular function, service, collection of data, or information asset does not justify the cost of implementing and maintaining the controls" (Whitman & Mattord, 2017). While accepting some risk is normal, permitting serious risks to go unfixed is not acceptable and eventually leads to terrible ramifications; the consequences Adult Friend Finder had to endure because of the security breach included a severe monetary loss that the organization will continuously struggle to recover from, a loss of their customer base, and a loss of their reputation. That is why completely disregarding the need for effective information security and the technology needed to secure a network is far from prudent. From now on, it would be safe to assume that Adult Friend Finder will address both their threats and potential threats in a more effective manner, they will take those vulnerabilities into account, and they will make threat assessments so that they can implement a solid game plan that will protect them from the most devastating attacks. Even though this was a terrible situation, if Adult Friend Finder's security breach sheds more light on the importance of information security, then at least some good came from tragedy.

References

Cluley, G. (2016, November 14). AdultFriendFinder data breach –

what you need to know. Retrieved April 5, 2018, from

Tripwire: https://www.tripwire.com/state-of-

security/featured/adultfriendfinder-data-breach-what-you-

need-to-know/

Gibbs, S. (2016, November 14). Adult Friend Finder and Penthouse

hacked in massive personal data breach. Retrieved April 5,

2018, from The Guardian:

https://www.theguardian.com/technology/2016/nov/14/adu

lt-friend-finder-and-penthouse-hacked-in-largest-personal-

data-breach-on-record

Lima, D. (2016, November 21). Lessons to be learned from Adult

FriendFinder hack of 412M accounts. Retrieved April 5, 2018,

from South Florida Business Journal:

https://www.bizjournals.com/southflorida/news/2016/11/21

/lessons-to-be-learned-from-adult-friendfinder-hack.html

OWASP. (2015, August 3). OWASP Testing Guide v4. Retrieved

April 5, 2018, from OWASP.org:

https://www.owasp.org/images/1/19/OTGv4.pdf

Peterson, A. (2016, Novemeber 14). Adult FriendFinder hit with

one of the biggest data breaches ever, report says. Retrieved

April 5, 2018, from Washington Post:

https://www.washingtonpost.com/news/the-

switch/wp/2016/11/14/adult-friendfinder-hit-with-one-of-

the-biggest-data-breaches-ever-report-says/?noredirect=on&utm_term=.6cff6705fcb6

Ragan, S. (2016, N🅰ovember 13). 412 million FriendFinder accounts exposed by hackers. Retrieved April 5, 2018, from CSO:

https://www.csoonline.com/article/3139311/security/412-million-friendfinder-accounts-exposed-by-hackers.html

Riley, S. (2006, February 14). Password Security: What Users Know and What They Actually Do. Retrieved April 5, 2018, from Usability News:

http://citeseerx.ist.psu.edu/viewdoc/download?doi=10.1.1.5 97.5846&rep=rep1&type=pdf

Storm, D. (2016, November 14). Biggest hack of 2016: 412 million FriendFinder Networks accounts exposed. Retrieved April 5, 2018, from Computerworld:

https://www.computerworld.com/article/3141290/security/ biggest-hack-of-2016-412-million-friendfinder-network-accounts-exposed.html

Whitman, M., & Mattord, H. (2017). Management of Information Security. Retrieved April 5, 2018, from VitalSource Bookshelf:

https://bookshelf.vitalsource.com/books/9781337520171

Whittaker, Z. (2016, November 21). AdultFriendFinder network finally comes clean to members about hack. Retrieved April 5, 2018, from ZDNet:

https://www.zdnet.com/article/adultfriendfinder-finally-

comes-clean-with-users-about-site-hacks/

Whittaker, Z. (2016, November 13). AdultFriendFinder network

hack exposes 412 million accounts. Retrieved April 5, 2018,

from ZDNet:

https://www.zdnet.com/article/adultfriendfinder-network-

hack-exposes-secrets-of-412-million-users/

9

MYSPACE

By: William "Cody" Harris

Like the bellbottoms trend of the 70's, big hair in the 80's, and grunge rock of the 90's, the social networking site Myspace was all the rage in the early 2000's. It is likely that you yourself even had a Myspace page, if you fit into that 18 to 25 year old range during the time. As one of the pioneers of the social media epidemic, Myspace lured in the new generation of young adults with the promise of a place of your own, where you were free to express yourself and meet new and likeminded individuals. Now, a decade and a half later, those long forgotten Myspace accounts may be coming back to haunt those 18 to 25 year olds, now in their late 20's and 30's, have graduated college and moved on in life to become working professionals. You might be thinking to yourself, "So what? Why do I care if hackers broke into a Myspace account that I haven't used in 10 years?", but your personality quizzes and party night photos are not the concern here. Hackers see these accounts as the perfect opportunity to take advantage of unsuspecting users with poor password hygiene.

According to an untitled blog post by Myspace, in May of 2016 they discovered that a large amount of user data, mainly email accounts, usernames, and passwords, were being sold on the dark web (MySpace, 2016). They go on to explain that the only affected accounts were those created prior to June 11, 2013 when, in an effort to enhance security, Myspace relaunched the site with new and more stringent account security requirements (Weise, 2016). Though it is unknown exactly when this breach occurred, or the time frame in which data was being exfiltrated from the company, the dates associated with this event suggests that hackers may have had access to this data for quite some time.

In all, 427 million passwords were compromised affecting as many as 360 million Myspace users, making it the fourth largest data breach in history to date (Palermo & Wagenseil, 2017). Myspace indicated that they believe that the Russian hacker "Peace_of_Mind", or more commonly known as "Peace", was responsible for the breach (MySpace, 2016). In an interview with Wired magazine, "Peace" does in fact claim responsibility for the event, stating that he made nearly $20,000 from the combined sale of Myspace and Tumblr data he had stolen (Greenberg, 2016).

As of 2016, "Peace" and his team of hackers can be linked to more than 800 million compromised user accounts from not only Myspace, but other company's like LinkedIn, Twitter, Tumblr, and the Russian social media site VK. One might think to themselves, "How could user credentials from a social media site that hasn't been relevant in more than 10 years, be worth anything to anyone?", but as "Peace" points out in his interview with Wired, password reuse is what makes these seemingly valueless bits of data actually worth something (Greenberg, 2016). The idea that users, for the sake of convenience, often reuse credentials across a myriad of social networks, finance, and communication sites, is not lost on the hackers that make their living profiting off of oblivious internet users.

A recent survey conducted by LogMein of 2,000 individuals spanning 5 major tech-dependent countries, showed that 59% of people reuse credentials across multiple online accounts. This same survey showed that 79% of those users surveyed owned between one and twenty online accounts for either professional or personal use (Vijayan, 2018). Given some rough math and a degree of approximation assuming each of those users had the maximum 20 accounts each, this would suggest that of the 360 million user accounts that were compromised, more than 212 million users potentially reused these credentials across as many as 3.4 billion online accounts. Though this is a worst case scenario number, it gives rise to the concerns that password and credential reuse is a staggering, yet profitable, issue. This shows how a single account compromise has the potential to open up a whole new level of attack surface for one individual.

While the exact method used to breach Myspace systems remains unknown, we do know of some security failures that made this data more enticing. In the interview with Wired magazine, "Peace" explained that Myspace did not salt their password hashes, making the stolen data even more valuable, and no, he is not referring to that delicious, high sodium seasoning being sprinkled across your hash browns (Greenberg, 2016).

Hashing is actually a form of one-way encryption used to scramble password data so that it is unreadable to humans (Greenburg , 2016). Like most security technology, however, hashing has been beaten by opposing technology and is no longer enough on its own, especially for companies with the responsibility to protect their user's data. In the case of the Myspace breach, in reference to the password data "Peace" explained, "Yes, it was hashed, however no salt", indicating that he was likely able to reverse the hash process (Greenberg, 2016).

Salting hashes adds a layer of complexity that makes it considerably harder for hackers to reverse the hash process and obtain actual password data. Salting is the addition of a secret, random generation of bits added to the end of a password before hashing, effectively lengthening the complexity of the password hash and making it much harder for hackers to reverse (Stewart, Chapple, & Gibson, 2015). Had Myspace salted their hashed passwords, it is likely that the user credentials that were stolen would never have been useable, or at least not before Myspace had time to inform their users of the breach and how to properly protect themselves against the fallout.

So where do we go from here? The Myspace response was not to worry, they've got you covered, "In order to protect our users, we have invalidated all user passwords for the affected accounts created prior to June 11, 2013 on the old Myspace platform" (MySpace, 2016). Great news! You can rest assured that your Myspace account that you last used in 2010, is safe! As for the other 15 plus social media, email, banking, and shopping sites you used those exact same credentials for so that you didn't have to wear out the "Forgot Password" button, you might want to start panicking right about now.

In a less than security minded turn of events, Myspace, in response to this massive security breach, hammered down on their password protection process. By moving to the use of double salted hashes, user passwords were now considerably more protected than they ever had before (Galloway, 2017). There was just one tiny problem. Though Myspace had upped its password encryption game, it missed a comically huge vulnerability in their account recovery process.

Cyber security researcher Leigh-Anne Galloway, inadvertently discovered a major flaw in the Myspace account recovery process when she went to delete her own long forgotten account. Because it has been such a long time since she had used the account she had to use the account recovery process to gain access to her account before she could delete it. This is when she realized that in order to recover her account she needed only very little information; her name, username, and birth date. While this doesn't seem to be completely unreasonable for an account recovery process, the real problem lies in the fact that there was no account validation or lockout process implemented to protect against brute force attacks (Galloway, 2017).

Taking this mockery of security one step further, there is no input validation for required fields of the account recovery process. This means that fields marked as "required" are not actually required, and because this process doesn't use an email account validation process either, you can simply input any email address your choose to move on in the process. What this really boils down to, is that if you were a hacker pursuing Myspace pages you wanted to compromise, you would only need one piece of information from your identified target in order to take ownership of their account, their date of birth. This is because the other two pieces of information you need are listed right on the front of the target's Myspace page, the name and username, which is located in the profile url. At this point all a hacker needs is to identify the target's date of birth, which could likely be found without too much trouble, otherwise a brute force attack would do the trick in no time at all (Galloway, 2017).

Myspace has since corrected the errors on the account recovery page and implemented much stronger password protection criteria to protect their users against breaches like the one disclosed in 2016. This being said, the moral of our story is that protection against online security mishaps is often up to the user, and not the organization. In many cases, the organization will do what is necessary to protect their systems, but they cannot protect the user against themselves. Being aware of poor password hygiene as a realistic threat as well as the actions you can take to protect yourself, is your own responsibility.

References

Myspace (May 31, 2016). Myspace.com. [Online] May 31 , 2016.
https://myspace.com/pages/blog.

Weise, E. (May, 2016). 360 Million Myspace Accounts Breached.
usatoday. [Online] May 31, 2016.
https://www.usatoday.com/story/tech/2016/05/31/360-

million-myspace-accounts-breached/85183200/.

Palermo, E. and Wagenseil, P. (2017). The Worst Data Breaches of
All Time. tomsguide.com. [Online] October 3, 2017.
https://www.tomsguide.com/us/pictures-story/872-worst-
data-breaches.html#s3.

Greenberg, A. (July, 2016). An Interview with the Hacker Probably
Selling Your Password Right Now. www.wired.com. [Online]
June 9, 2016. https://www.wired.com/2016/06/interview-
hacker-probably-selling-password/.

Vijayan, J. (2018). Password Reuse Abounds, New Survey Shows.
www.darkreading.com. [Online] May 1, 2018.
https://www.darkreading.com/informationweek-
home/password-reuse-abounds-new-survey-shows/d/d-
id/1331689.

Greenburg, A. (2016). Hacker Lexicon: What is Password Hashing.
www.wired.com. [Online] June 8, 2016.
https://www.wired.com/2016/06/hacker-lexicon-password-
hashing/.

Stewart, J., Chapple, M., and Gibson, D. (2015). Certified
Information Sytems Security Professional Study Guide (7th
ed.). Indianapolis, IN : John Wiley & Sons, Inc., 2015.

Galloway, L. (2017). It's not Yourspace, it's Myspace. www.leigh-
annegalloway.com. [Online] July 17, 2017. https://leigh-
annegalloway.com/myspace/.

10

TUMBLR

By: Jeff Falcon

Tumblr, a popular website where users connect, share, discover and bond with people of similar interests, prides themselves on their simplicity and ease of use with their technology. "We made it really, really simple for people to make a blog and put whatever they want on it. Stories, photos, GIF's, TV shows, links, quips, dumb jokes, smart jokes, Spotify tracks, mp3s, videos, fashion, art, deep stuff. Tumblr is 425 million different blogs, filled with literally whatever" (Tumblr, 2018).

Unfortunately, this lively, creative and interactive haven for connecting people and their interests fell victim to a data breach in 2013 reportedly compromising over 65 million accounts that were hosted for sale on the dark web. In early 2016, security researcher Troy Hunt, (owner of the website Haveibeenpwned), located a database of the compromised information that was posted for sale by a hacker known as "Peace". The database was being sold for $150 (Motherboard, 2016).

As data breaches will surely continue to increase, many organizations lack the immediate resources and overall ability to notify their customers of a breach until long after it has occurred. This exposes individuals to further attacks that they may be susceptible to falling victim toward. Individuals potentially are afforded a better fighting chance of minimizing the damage accrued if they are given early warning indications to reset their credentials across their accounts in order to better protect themselves. The sharing and the re-use of the same passwords across personal accounts (iCloud, Twitter, Gmail, etc.) and other related domains is a serious risk. The Tumblr breach perpetuates and cascades this effort according to Hunt. "There is a massive trade in stolen data, liking it to the collection of baseball cards. These people might not necessarily have any malicious interest in the data itself, but simply collect, swap and archive data sets" (Motherboard, 2016).

Although little is known about the exact specifics behind the Tumblr breach, it is suspected that Tumblr had a vulnerability that allowed the attacker to dump a user database without any use of malware to penetrate the victim network. The findings and lessons learned from the Tumblr data breach may help encourage organizations to take a broader look at holistic, synchronized security strategies.   Synchronized security may also be related to the process of improving the operational efficiencies of an organization's IT processes.

The market is currently flooded with an abundance of cybersecurity tools. This complex ecosystem of products is difficult to manage and maintain holistically, even for seasoned and mature security organizations. There is an overwhelming amount of technical innovations, process changes, and business drivers that create overlaps and gaps within any given organization's security product investments. This ongoing dilemma forces organizations to continually assess and test their current stack of controls to ensure they are delivering value as originally intended.

We may think of synchronized security in several ways, as it potentially delivers better results toward the identification and response procedures toward an attack. Another way to view synchronized security is automation and orchestration of tools. "In addition to saving time and energy, this also leads to quicker incident resolutions and frees up an IT team/Security staff to focus on harder problems like detecting advanced threats (Levy, 2018). Analyzing this concept further, synchronized security automates the response in method that limits an attacker's ability to continue their advance on a victim network. Operating under the assumption that the Tumblr breach started with an attacker dumping credentials and using that information to access data within the organization, tools that deliver automated machine learning (ML) based technologies could play a key role in disrupting this effort by detecting and blocking the attempted credential dump. Designing and architecting a strategy that supports synchronized security plays a vital role in correlating and analyzing data across critical enclaves of an IT environment (endpoints, servers, access points and firewalls) to name a few. According to Levy, "the more you can see what's happening across devices, the better context you have to identify and understand advanced threats. Synchronization allows security teams to coordinate a response across different control points, not just at the point of a single detection, but rather completely disrupts an attempted breach across its various stages" (Levy, 2018).

References

Motherboard. Franceschi-Bicchierai, Lorenzo. Hackers Stole 65 Million Passwords From Tumblr, New Analysis Reveals. May 30, 2016. https://motherboard.vice.com/en_us/article/8q88k5/hackers-stole-68-million-passwords-from-tumblr-new-analysis-reveals

Hunt, Troy. Check if you have an account that has been compromised in a data breach. 2018.

https://haveibeenpwned.com

Sophos, Naked Security. 2018.https://nakedsecurity.sophos.com/

Levy, Joe. Chief Technology Officer, Sophos. Personal
Communication. 2018.https://www.sophos.com/en-
us/company/management/joe-levy.aspx

11

NSA SHADOW BROKERS

By: Mary Knapp

The WannaCry ransomware attack of 2017 hit the media like a wildfire when the vulnerability was first discovered. News reports warned the public that a Microsoft Windows flaw, if not patched, would allow an attacker to access their computer and inject a crypto worm. A crypto worm is a type of virus that is programmed to find a pathway and spread to as many computers as it can gain access to, ultimately looking for a machine or server that houses sensitive data or even critical systems. In the case of WannaCry, when the worm found data, it encrypted the information, rendering it unusable until a key is entered to unlock the information. The attackers only provide this key after paying a ransom. There is no guarantee that paying the ransom will allow for recovery of the encrypted data.

The reason that WannaCry was a big news story when it was first discovered is that it targeted a specific vulnerability in

Microsoft Windows. According to research done by the online company, Net Marketshare, Microsoft Windows runs on over 80% of the computers, servers, and mobile devices around the world. That equates to over a billion devices (Warren, 2017). The possibility of being infected was high, and the likelihood that the infection would hit a major company or industry was a certainty.

Experts estimate that over 200,000 computers across more than 150 countries were infected by WannaCry, including healthcare systems around the world. In the U.K. alone, more than a third of their healthcare facilities were affected. Healthcare systems across the globe were forced to cancel appointments, and, in some cases, sensitive medical equipment was rendered unusable leaving the hospitals unable to provide services to their patients (Seals, 2018).

Who would build an exploit like WannaCry, and why?

The answer to this begins in 2013 when the clandestine hacking group, the Shadow Brokers, gained access to a National Security Agency (NSA) server and stole the NSA's hacking tools. Among the tools were exploits for various software and hardware device vulnerabilities. The stolen data also contained a list of feats that could be used against Microsoft Windows (Schneir, 2017). The NSA's hacking experts, known as Tailored Access

Operations (TAO), are probably the most elite hacking group in the world. They gather these exploits either to conduct ongoing operations or for future national security applications. Among the Microsoft exploits was a piece of code called Eternalblue.

Eternalblue is an exploit that was developed by the National Security Agency to take advantage of a Microsoft Windows vulnerability. It was in the treasure trove of exploits the NSA hoarded and subsequently had stolen in 2013 by the Shadow Brokers. This exploit was used to build the WannaCry ransomware used in the 2017 attacks (Khandelwal, 2017). However, it wasn't the Shadow Brokers who created and distributed WannaCry, but rather, unknown attackers who purchased and then used the Eternalblue exploit after receiving it from the Shadow Brokers.

How did the WannaCry authors receive the Eternalblue exploit?

After the 2013 hack of the NSA servers, the Shadow Brokers sat on the information for three years. They made no announcement of themselves or the information they acquired until August of 2016 when they went public and promised to share or sell the NSA's secrets. Asking for payment in ZEC, or Zcash, the group started a dump service, which is a leak of exploits that would be made available at the beginning of each month. Later, they also launched a VIP service which would allow someone to pay for a specific exploit. That service started at 400 ZEC, which equates to $131,000. In their signature broken English, the Shadow Brokers stated: "VIP Service is no guarantee of future good or services, negotiation for those is being separate." (Shane, Perloth, Sanger, 2017). The Shadow Brokers occasionally released information to the public at no cost, leaving experts puzzled by their behavior. It wasn't clear until their identity was revealed, why the Shadow Brokers would wait three years to release information, or why some of their information leaks were free of charge. Eternalblue was part of the monthly paid service released the month before the WannaCry attacks.

Prior to the Shadow Brokers release of Eternalblue, the NSA became aware that the exploit had been stolen. According to a former cybersecurity official at the Pentagon, Mike McNerny, the "NSA identified a risk and communicated it to Microsoft, who put out an immediate patch." After learning of the vulnerability, Microsoft canceled their scheduled February patch release, dubbed "Patch Tuesday," for the first time in the company's history. Microsoft released the patch a month later, but the Eternalblue leak came less than a month after the patch release. Without a press release or public warning to raise awareness of the new patch, many users remained vulnerable until when the WannaCry attack was launched (Goodin, 2017). Only those with vigilant patching schedules were able to protect themselves in time.

Who are the Shadow Brokers, and how did they hack the NSA?

Initially, the Shadow Brokers' identity was unknown, causing much speculation amongst experts. We now know they are a Russian intelligence group (Schindler, 2018). Concerned more with embarrassing the NSA than profiting from the exploits, Russian intelligence chose to go public with the NSA tools rather than hoard the exploits to use for their own gain. They were able to access information deeply guarded inside the National Security Agency through espionage, ironically, via the well-known anti-malware software, Kaspersky (Kelley, 2018). Kaspersky, a software company headquartered in Moscow, Russia, produces an anti-virus/anti-malware software package used globally on over 400 million machines. The nature of any anti-virus software is to have access to all files on a computer so that it can scan for malicious code. However, the point of this type of software is to guard against malware, not act as a trojan horse.

Kaspersky denies the accusation that their software was used to compromise the NSA, but U.S. intelligence officials have indicated that this is indeed the case. Experts agree and warn skeptics that there is no way to prove the allegation without revealing their source (Kelley, 2018). It's widely accepted among government officials, professional experts, and the general public that Russian intelligence is behind the Shadow Brokers hack.

Can the NSA protect us if they can't defend themselves?

When it came to light that the NSA was responsible for creating this exploit, the public was not only outraged that they did not publicize the possibility of the attack, but they were also extremely disillusioned with the NSA's ability to protect national secrets if they could not even protect their own information. The hack was embarrassing to the NSA, damaging to those attacked by the stolen exploits, and continues to cause problems as agencies try to retrieve exploits that have yet to be released. But that doesn't mean that the NSA can't protect us as a nation.

What the public may not understand about cybersecurity is that you cannot create a system that is attacker-proof. No matter the security controls in place, there's always a way to steal, damage, or destroy information. You can put a server behind a firewall logically and a locked door physically, but there are ways to penetrate firewalls and locked doors. Cybersecurity is all about risk and mitigation. Every person or organization must accept some level of risk to operate a computer or information system. If a company wants to have a server based architecture for file sharing, the risk of sharing a computer virus is also introduced. Rather than using computers to share files, papers could be passed from office to office. However, this isn't a feasible solution and even then, a fire could burn down the building and all of the papers. Therefore, you never remove risk. It will always exist in some capacity.

You can mitigate risk to an acceptable level. Let the users have connected computers, but limit the scope of their reach with various technological measures, including firewalls and switches. For instance, if you use subnets, "broadcast attacks can be stopped at switches, but directed attacks would need protection between subnets" which would mean using firewalls (D. Bazluke, personal communication, June 25, 2018). This configuration stops a virus from spreading to a different subnet because it eliminates a method of traversal. If you add intrusion detection systems (IDS) and/or intrusion prevention systems (IPS), risk is reduced even more. These choices depend on your need and your budget. But, no matter how many layers of security you add, you will never have 100% protection against threats. The best anyone can do is to mitigate risks to an acceptable level.

It just isn't feasible to believe that any government agency is 100% protected against an attack. The bigger the target each agency represents, the more attacks they can expect. Regardless of the method, anyone can be hacked at any time, whether that be a pure cyber-attack, or perhaps a blend of physical and cyber-attack. Even a person walking out the door with classified papers in their briefcase presents a risk to agencies with national security information. Do I believe that the NSA is incapable of protecting the secrets of the United States because they got hacked? No, I truly don't. Do I think they are an inviting target and will be breached again? Yes. But in my educated opinion, I believe they will have procedures in place to avoid the same thing from happening again. Attackers will have to be much craftier in the future. Hopefully, the NSA will stay a step ahead of them.

Is it okay for the NSA to hold on to exploits rather than notifying the companies of their vulnerabilities and allowing them to release a patch? They can create custom exploits in-house, but what about the vulnerabilities they find in commercial software and hardware? When the NSA finds a weakness and creates an exploit for it, they save it for their own use without notifying the software developer. With notice from the NSA, patches for known vulnerabilities could be created proactively, but instead must wait until the exploits appear in the wild. This type of cyber warfare raises a lot of questions about ethics, procedures, and law.

Take this scenario for instance: If the NSA exploits a vulnerability found in a popular piece of software and uses that exploit to spy on those that would bring harm to others, I find that to be acceptable *as long as* they take action on the threat intel. If they sit on the info for fear of revealing their source and wishing to use the breach for longer at the cost of others' lives or resources, I think they have lost the honor in their actions. They also need to weigh the benefit vs the risk that someone else will find the same vulnerability and use it against the people. Case-in-point: Eternalblue.

The NSA gambled that holding on to Eternalblue would pay off for them if they ever needed a global reach on sensitive systems, but they weren't counting on losing control of that information. They also risked ill-intentioned people finding that vulnerability first. The NSA hope was that if they ever needed EternalBlue, they could use it to aid in national security. For instance, if the United States wanted to cripple the nuclear control systems of a nation state threatening nuclear launch, it would be to our advantage to have this type of resource in our arsenal. Or perhaps if we needed intel on a foreign group planning to attack our President, Eternalblue would have been our ally. Unfortunately, that's not what happened. Still, some would argue that holding on to this type of information is worth the risk. Others would have the NSA inform companies of the security hole and patch their vulnerabilities as soon as possible to protect the people, even though it would eliminate a method of attack. Without a crystal ball to see into the future, it's hard to know what the right call is.

The best we can do is hope the NSA secures its data and recovers the remains of their lost information while bringing justice to those who stole our information and those who used it to attack others. We are at cyberwar with many enemies at all times, and I predict things will only get more complex in the future.

References

Goodin, D., Lurkius, S., Fitz, I., W., UTC, & Ars Centurion. (2017, May 17). Fearing Shadow Brokers leak, NSA reported critical flaw to Microsoft. Retrieved from https://arstechnica.com/information-technology/2017/05/fearing-shadow-brokers-leak-nsa-reported-critical-flaw-to-microsoft/

Goodin, D., & UTC. (2017, April 14). NSA-leaking Shadow Brokers just dumped its most damaging release yet. Retrieved from https://arstechnica.com/information-technology/2017/04/nsa-leaking-shadow-brokers-just-dumped-its-most-damaging-release-yet/

Kelley, M. (2018, January 13). 'Very high level of confidence' Russia used Kaspersky software for devastating NSA leaks. Retrieved from https://finance.yahoo.com/news/experts-link-nsa-leaks-shadow-brokers-russia-kaspersky-144840962.html

Khandelwal, S. (2017, September 08). Shadow Brokers Leaks Another Windows Hacking Tool Stolen from NSA's Arsenal. Retrieved from https://thehackernews.com/2017/09/shadowbrokers-unitedrake-hacking.html

Schindler, J. (18, February 13). American Spies Get Fooled by the Kremlin Again. Retrieved from http://observer.com/2018/02/nsa-spies-seeking-shadow-brokers-secrets-fooled-by-kremlin-new-york-times/

Seals, T. (2018, June 25). WannaCry Extortion Fraud Reemerges. Retrieved from https://threatpost.com/wannacry-extortion-fraud-reemerges/133062/

Shane, S., Perlroth, N., & Sanger, D. E. (2017, November 12). Security Breach and Spilled Secrets Have Shaken the N.S.A. to Its Core. Retrieved from https://www.nytimes.com/2017/11/12/us/nsa-shadow-brokers.html

Warren, T. (2017, April 4). Apple reveals Windows 10 is fourtimes more popular than the Mac. Retrieved from https://www.theverge.com/2017/4/4/15176766/apple-microsoft-windows-10-vs-mac-users-figures-stats

12

CLINTON EMAIL

By: Manny Bamba

The fundamental underpinnings of Clinton's email issues may vary, depending sometimes on political views or leanings of the professional and casual observers. However, the facts established on the ground by the FBI after its investigations of the matter based on a referral from the US Intelligence Community Inspector General (ICIG), can help clarify the crucial aspects and events of this sometimes muddied water of Clinton's email controversy. Moreover, various investigative reporting by journalists in leading news outlets such as New York Times, Politico and New Yorker magazine among many, have also helped confirm accounts and events that transformed the Clinton's emails controversy into a full blown crisis that would ultimately impact the Presidential election of 2016. Consequently, the question must be asked what was the Clinton's emails controversy about? Why was it relevant to the national discourse relating to

the 2016 Presidential election and the US national security ?
Essentially, the key aspects of the controversy involve the
deployment by Clinton and her aides of a private network
infrastructure (i.e. Own domain clintonemail.com) to handle her
emails, the attempted or ensuing hackings via spear phishing (e.g.
use of fake links obtained via deceptive email solicitations and
redirecting to a bogus web site in order to steel or collect
credentials from legitimate owners) that took place and alleged
potential impact on the US National Security (i.e. Potential
compromise of information by hostile actors including foreign
adversaries) while Clinton was Secretary of the State. In effect,
the Clinton's email server controversy invites or compels the
casual and interested observers to view and assess the crucial
aspects of potential mishandling of national secrets in both sent
and received emails, vulnerabilities and risks posed by the
deployed private network infrastructure including its
management in the context of possible noncompliance with the
law relating to the Federal Records Act.

In essence, the ICIG referral was in regard to potential
unauthorized transmission and storage of classified information
on the former Secretary of State Clinton's personal email server.
So in the retrospect, did Clinton's email server practices
potentially compromise the US national security and underlying
handling procedures? Were the deployed security

countermeasures appropriate to secure the infrastructure ? And finally, was there any law broken in the process regarding the information classification and federal record retention requirements ? At close look, these enumerated points seem more fundamental and pronounced in Clinton's email server issues or controversy than the related attempted or active hackings directed at the email server. During its deployment life cycle, the server infrastructure underwent various upgrades, first, it was installed in the Clinton's residence in Chappaqua New York and then moved to Equinix co-location facilities in Secaucus New Jersey. Incidentally, the cyber-attacks in terms of successful hacks turned out to be very limited based on the FBI forensic analysis and assessment (AP, 2018). Operationally, the controversy also highlighted how potential misuse of technology either intentionally or unintentionally combined with inadequate enforcement of security awareness practices in turn underlie by lax compliance with the appropriate system operations and governance frameworks could cascade and escalate into a public relation nightmare as they became for the presidential candidate and then Secretary of State Clinton. In this context, the chronology of the unfolding events that underpinned the Clinton's email issues gives the readers a comprehensive understanding of what happened, the rationale behind deploying a private network infrastructure, hackings that exploited information or attempted

to compromise those data and their ultimate impact on the
presidential election of 2016 that pitted Clinton against Trump. In
terms of the system operations and its use, as described by
Politico (politico.com) and in the FBI investigation including
forensic analysis, Secretary Clinton mainly relied on personal
devices such as iPad's and preferred blackberry phones supported
by a loyal inner circle of advisers like Huma Abedin, Sheryl Mills
her chief of staff, Justin Cooper and Bryan Pagliano among others
to handle most of her email communications needs and
infrastructure (Gass, 2016).

Technology Environment at the US State Department

As commonly understood and practiced, a system Acceptable
Use Policy (AUP) is an integral component of an organization
overall Security Program in protecting its vital assets in support of
its stated mission. In this context, an evaluation of Clinton's email
system infrastructure had to be done in part based on the
assessment whether it violated or complied with the Security
policy in effect at the time of the networks interconnecting or
interacting including their use while she was Secretary of the
State. Moreover, it is further understood that information about
the US National Defense and Foreign Relations potentially require
classification for protection against unauthorized disclosure (i.e.
Executive Order 13526). Against this backdrop, the reported
experiences of State Department own employees in related

investigations and reporting (Politico, 2016) suggested that the technology infrastructure seemed inadequate, presenting to the readers a picture of legacy and cumbersome IT system that was not providing timely services.

For example, in illustrating the technology environment shortcomings at the Department of the State (DOS), Politico alluded to the fact that even Colin Powell, the former Secretary of State before Clinton found only an outdated single laptop on his desk as his main access computer (Gass, 2016). Moreover, this investigative reporting highlighted that the majority of the people working at the DOS found that the email system was difficult to work with due to its slowness and complicated handling process of classified and unclassified documents. For these reasons among many others, the FBI and other reports suggested that most of the DOS employees had also come to rely on personal emails accounts such as Gmail to conduct partially their official duties. So, even though not officially sanctioned, the use of personal accounts had become an implicitly accepted culture by many employees to supplement the official DOS network for their daily tasks. Consequently, rigorously designed document handling protocols were routinely circumvented for convenience and ease of use. For improvement, it is believed at some point that Collin Powell in his tenure as Secretary made a quick decision to buy around 44,000 brand new computers to remedy the deficiency and ineffective technical operational environment that was prevalent at DOS (Gass, 2016). In this context, these operational constraints may have contributed as well to the Clinton's reliance on her email server, as she depended on her trusted blackberry devices which were not authorized for use at DOS and an accommodating process had to be found or implemented for her to function effectively as Secretary of State. As anecdotally reported, Clinton had various upgraded devices (e.g. Ipad's) provided to her along the way, but always resorted or fell back to her blackberry she was comfortable with. Additionally, prior to Clinton tenure, Secretary Powell had also fired the entire IT people working at the DOS and turned its infrastructure management over to the CIA with much more rigorous document handling protocols in trying to fix or unify the operational environment technical support.

Background of the server setup.

From the view points of the FBI investigation, including that of close aides and those around her, Clinton did not understand the technical details about the network infrastructure that was powering or delivering her emails as she basically concerned herself with the use of the front end devices such as the iPad's she received and along with her preferred blackberry phones not far away. As highlighted in various published reports and investigations, essentially, the first Clinton's email server was a remnant from equipment's (i.e. Apple Server) salvaged from her previous presidential campaign against President Obama. The desire to set up a server was the brain child of her aides and others in an attempt to consolidate and preserve her emails as she had lost prior information and data due to address changes and phone carriers upgrades among others after her lost in 2008 presidential bid to President Barak Obama. Subsequently, the system born out of this data consolidation and preservation process will follow her to the State Department as the tool of "convenience" to hold or transact the bulk of her email data and accounts during her tenure at DOS. And as stated in reports, the main architects of the Clinton's email system were Justin Cooper and Bryan Pagliano who later carried out or facilitated the required upgrades and other changes along the way (Gerstein, 2016).

Officially, Clinton became the Secretary of State in 2009 and the State Department technical support had the rule communicated to her that personal emails accounts were not allowed to be configured on the government issued devices. In the view of her aides as stated in reports, she was not comfortable with carrying two devices around. Thus, Secretary Clinton decided to stick with her active Blackberry device which was linked to her newly registered domain name clintonemail.com. In the early phase of the private server, Justin Cooper had taken on the job of figuring out how to find a server and set it up (New Yorker, 2006). This server setup ended up being staged on a recycled computer prior to Hillary becoming the Secretary of State. Broadly in 2008, the Clintons also had two additional domains: wjcoffice.com which was essentially for auto-forwarding to other accounts and presidentclinton.com used by President Clinton post presidency staff, all running on an Apple Server in their residence basement in Chappaqua New York. In the meantime, Hillary Clinton's own email accounts were carrier based such as hr15@mycingular.blackberry.net and hr15@att.blackberry.net after AT&T acquisition of Cingular network. Later on and with the help of a former IT staff member from her 2008 Presidential campaign Bryan Pagliano, an upgrade was also performed to change this recycled existing server in Chappaqua residence according to the FBI findings in its subsequent investigation. In the process of the setup undertaken, Clinton's aides Huma Abedin and Cooper agreed on the domain name clintonemail.com as well to handle their boss emails. As the setup was being completed in the following months in 2009, and for this server account to be globally accessible to its Internet users (i.e. Creating worldwide valid MX record for DNS resolution and mail delivery), Cooper also apparently registered the domain with Network Solutions as the registrar after Clinton's nomination as the Secretary of State by President Barack Obama. In effect, Clinton became the 67th Secretary of State occupying as many other prior US government principals leading the US Foreign Policy, the 7th floor office at the DOS also referred to as "Mahogany Row" by its people.

The Clinton's emails and the following FBI investigation

The subsequent FBI investigations and forensic analysis released a report with some redacted pages (e.g. For prevention of unauthorized disclosures) and interview notes of the events that led to the email controversy from Clinton's tenure as Secretary of State and during her 2016 run for the presidency of the United States. In conducting its investigations, the FBI interviewed various actors from the former Secretary of State Colin Powell, CIA officers to the IT staffers who first assembled the email server in the Clinton's home in Chappaqua New York. The established report also contained the forensic analysis results, details and rational (i.e. Stated reasons of emails data consolidation, preservation and convenience for access) of the staff decision to setup the email server along with the adopted system architecture. Furthermore, the report along with other investigative findings by news outlets explained with some confirmations why Clinton did cling to her trusted Blackberry and highlighted the sometimes confusing and cumbersome DOS processes that fostered or exacerbated the emails issues. Additionally during its investigation, the FBI also talked to both Clinton's opponents and supporters including other neutral parties of civil servants in and outside of State Department. In effect, with all these various actors in combination with the 302's (i.e. the summary reports by trained FBI agent), the bureau established a more comprehensive view of the email server controversy. Essentially, during her tenure as the Secretary of State, for about five years, Clinton's email server and varying upgrades stayed operational in her home in Chappaqua New York and was later moved into Equinix data center in Secaucus New Jersey. Ultimately in the end, the email issues did maintain a cloud of doubt and inconclusive determinations (e.g. Due to some potentially unrecovered or missing devices contents by the FBI) over Clinton's US presidential run in the election of 2016 which ended in her defeat by Donald Trump to become the President of the United States.

Clinton's Blackberry Device.

Since Blackberry was not allowed on the 7th floor or "Mahogany Row" as referenced earlier as matter of underlying policies or procedural restrictions among others, the DOS logistic people explored various options to accommodate Secretary Clinton for her to function effectively in her role as the head of US diplomacy. For example, it is worth noting that an accommodation had been done in the past for one of her predecessors like Colin Powell according to the FBI investigation. The DOS logistic people then looked at setting up a secure living room for the purpose of facilitating her communications but retained in the end the option for Clinton to leave her blackberry in a drawer at the diplomatic security station outside of her office. So, whenever Clinton needed to use her trusted blackberry, she would have to retrieve it and move around outside of her office. Faced with these type of procedural rules may be due to potential or unspecified vulnerabilities, the FBI investigation and other reports highlighted that Clinton casually reached out to Secretary Powell to get a sense on how he dealt with his own case constraints during his time at the DOS. Reportedly, Powell provided Clinton with his take on the matter and especially urged her to resist these "bureaucratic rules" in subtle and wise ways in order to be effective by not revealing too much and "avoiding unnecessary paper trails". As understood, Secretary Powell had asked the CIA and NSA during his own tenure about the restriction or inability to use PDA's with no satisfactory answers as far as he was concerned. Contextually, the alleged Clinton's conversation with Mr Powell could not be reasonably construed if ever as the all determining factor in her use of personal emails at the DOS. But rather as an element among many others in converging events underscoring the Clinton's email controversy. Given her known preference and reliance on her Blackberry devices based on the available reports.

The Email Server Infrastructure.

In March 2009, Bryan Pagliano was now working for the Department of State addressing mobile computing among others, had also assembled and upgraded the email server along with Cooper. As understood, Pagliano had also raised some security concerns about the server installation in Clinton's Chappaqua residence location (e.g. Fbi reports). But unlike Pagliano, Cooper preferred this basement location to the multivendor environment, suggesting that the private residence offered a more secure place from the increased likelihood of the system being subjected to potential exposure to security risks present in an openly accessible setting (e.g. Colocation or high traffic area with less restricted access). In effect, after the upgrade, the Chappaqua basement location was equipped with: a Kiwi Syslog server, Cisco private Internet exchange firewall and Windows Small Business server (i.e. Dell PoweEdge 1950) including

Blackberry Enterprise server to support the Clinton's preferred front end devices (e.g. iPad's and Blackberry phones). And the infrastructure security was later enhanced with SSL certificate. Additionally, in completing the upgrade, Pagliano migrated all the emails from the Apple Server onto the new setup with the old server being restaged for use as a desktop by the Clinton's household staff. Administratively, both Pagliano and Cooper maintained privileged access rights to the installed machines for maintenance and other administrative tasks.

Finally on March 18, 2009 Hillary is believed to have stopped using her carrier based email hr15@att.blackberry.net on the ATT network and switched to the new hrod17@clintonemail.com running on the new infrastructure. In the migration process, the case was made that the Clinton's old emails were lost including her first seven weeks of emails as Secretary of State. Distinctively later on, additional email accounts such as H@clintonemail.com was created by Cooper which would appear as the source of many emails forwarded to or sent from the private server account for Clinton in her correspondences with apparently no other information in the sender information field to the State Department recipients as confirmed by the people interviewed during the FBI investigation.

Using the new emails on the server

The upgrades of Clinton's Blackberry were regular and usually synched with the server by the staff. For example, her inner circle staff would enter information as needed and shared the related new password information with other close aides. Operationally, the executive secretariat's office of Information technology for the State Department top leadership also offered state.gov emails accounts to Clinton and those were allegedly declined by an inner circle aide familiar with Clinton's preference for personal email linked to her blackberry. However, exceptions were made to use smsgs@state.gov and sshrc@state.gov on her behave to send messages to all employees at the State Department and to manage the outlook calendar including scheduling meetings according to Politico and the FBI investigation. But, notably none of these emails accounts were used personally by Secretary Clinton.

According to the FBI findings and based on prevailing attitudes in the DOS at the time, Secretary Clinton's propensity to use personal email was not technically against the rules. In fact, for long time the practice of using personal email accounts has been tolerated if not implicitly accepted. However, caution was advised for security and compliance with record keeping requirement despite the apparent lack of restriction enforcement on using personal email accounts for official business. For example, forwarding work related emails to the employees official DOS established emails was seen or accepted as satisfying the requirement for retention. Thus, there was in effect no specific rule in place that prohibited Secretary Clinton's use of her private network supporting her email infrastructure. But despite the tolerated flexibility in operating, the DOS IG (i.e. Inspector General) emphasized internally that the use of private email was highly discouraged. Moreover, in its related findings and highlighting the persistent lax unofficial email accounts usage by many, the FBI director further confirmed that the security culture in general at DOS was lacking in regard to both unclassified and classified information when compared to other departments or areas in the US government.

Comparatively assessing Clinton's email issues within the security threat metrics context and required security awareness training needs, DOS Operational environment and assets security seemed relax as well at least at the time. Advisedly, a robust threat mitigation process should have been ongoing within a risk management framework for DOS to ensure Confidentiality, Integrity and Availability to its information assets. For example, in 2001 Colin Powell also had faced an outdated computer system environment. Consequently, he did deploy an unclassified email system for ease of use but preferred his own AOL account. Additionally, the "fob" system (i.e. key based authentication mechanism) deployed to make the DOS system easy for employees to access outside or remotely was viewed as too slow and prone to shutting down as referenced by the FBI investigation. Furthermore, underlying the going security requirement and concerns for interconnected networks in this digital age, in 2011 DOS also resorted to destroying about 30,000 of its fob keys and related credentials when they were hacked allegedly by Russian actors (Wall Street Journal, 2015). Collectively, it is assumed in nutshell that more than the majority of Clinton's emails traffic around sixty eight percent (68%) came from close aides like Ms Huma Abedin, Mills and Mr Sullivan among others. In essence per the FBI investigation in the email matter, very few people contacted Clinton directly beside family and the DOS executive leadership, for she mainly used her blackberry to text staff and send messages.

The Early Hacking Attempts Targeting Clinton Email Server.

The earliest observed and reported hacking attempts on Clinton's email server by Justin Cooper who was the co-administrator on the infrastructure occurred on around Jan 9, 2011. Reportedly, Cooper observed active brute force attacks on the server with repeated login attempts to overwhelm the system. And per available reports, Cooper apparently tried his best to stop the ongoing attacks. But in the end he physically powered down the server temporarily to halt the attacks taking place and was later trained on how to apply filters to block the offending or similar attacks source IPs as opposed to powering the server down manually. Obviously a hard power down would not be an ideal method in any operational environment sustaining a critical infrastructure with active servers. This particular hacking attempt did ultimately failed to penetrate the server. Understandably, several of these unobserved attack events had taken placed which were later confirmed by the FBI investigation as failed attacks or unsuccessful penetration attempts. Moreover, the monitoring software (i.e. Cloudjacket that was deployed) would also show several of the failed attacks with the FBI confirming that two iPad's belonging to Clinton herself had also been unsuccessfully targeted for penetration. In this context, one could also opine that Clinton reported restraint toward technology in general made her unknowingly a hard target for hackers to crack. Since Secretary Clinton was known to have hardly replied to no one avoiding in the process multiple random spear phishing attempts and a pornographic material believed to have been directed at her. However, unlike Clinton, some DOS employees accounts set up on Gmail and yahoo platforms were successfully hacked creating an ongoing security concerns throughout the DOS. Essentially, these attacks were perpetrated using phishing methods to change passwords and settings in order to auto-forward emails to the attackers or servers controlled by the intruders. Incidentally, it is notable that there was no encryption mechanism enabled on the email server such as TLS at the transport layer to provide some type of preemptive and ongoing protection to the Clinton's communication infrastructure server. In June 2011, Pagliano also would performed another upgrade to the server and network environment: he replaced the external drive, added more memory to the Dell server, a Gigabit switch, firewall, Cisco Botnet and an IPS system for Intrusion Prevention with required software patches hardening in the process the infrastructure environment against potential future attacks.

The Hack

Notwithstanding all the offensive penetration attempts by hackers and activities by both close aides and technical support team on Clinton's email server, in January 2013 the server was impacted by its first and only known successful hack or compromise that was acknowledged and confirmed by the FBI (Collinson & Kopan, 2016). Conversely, due to missing devices purportedly used by Secretary Clinton, the FBI could not conclusively state that no other potential successful hacks had not taken place since the server was put in operation. In effect, a member of the President Bill Clinton's staff email account on the server infrastructure was hacked via a TOR anonymizing software in and around Jan 5, 2013. Based on the forensic information assessment by the FBI, three known TOR IP addresses penetrated the server site and browsed thru this staffer account and attachments. But, the FBI was unable to identify the attackers and by the end of that month Clinton's tenure as the US Secretary of State had ended (Collinson & Kopan, 2016).. Effectively, Clinton resigned on Feb 1st 2013 and went back to private life.

Incidentally, about six weeks in the afterward of her departure from the State Department, on March 14th Guccifer viewed as an unsophisticated hacker and also a taxi driver by the name of " Marcel Lazar Lehel" cracked an email in which he found Sidney Blumenthal's email known to be among Clinton's close aides and confidants (Weiner & Hsu, 2016). It is alleged that another cracked email by the same attacker belonged to Colin Powell whose account had also been hacked. In subsequent conversation with the FBI, Guccifer told the Bureau that Blumenthal's email was relatively easy to cracked compared to the others such as that of a Romanian politician "Couna Cretu"(Weiner & Hsu, 2016). Essentially, Blumenthal's email password was just reset by the hacker in about twenty minutes by answering a security challenge question. By Guccifer own admission, he spent seven (7) hours browsing thru Blumenthal's email account of about 30,000 emails with other attachments including that of Benghazi and discovering in the process that Blumenthal regularly emailed Clinton(Weiner & Hsu, 2016). Moreover, Guccifer made several attempts to locate Clinton's email server unsuccessfully and eventually gave up. Realizing later that he had been locked out of his account, Mr Blumenthal is believed to have regained his access back by also resetting his password and thus halting at that point Guccifer free range access to his emails.

Since Guccifer habits were to send his findings to the media as he has similarly done, when he successfully hacked the Bush family and leaked George W. Bush's painting photos. Likewise, Guccifer sent Blumenthal's hacked emails to the media outlets exposing in the process Secretary Clinton's email domain "clintonemail.com" (Weiner & Hsu, 2016). In turns, this exposure created scanning frenzies against the email infrastructure server by hackers especially from the Russian and Romanian actors fingered based on the identified IP addresses along with other attackers attempting to gain access to the server. In effect, in the aftermath of this public exposure, Clinton's staff changed the email server address fearing data loss and other potential attacks on the infrastructure. Essentially, the exposure episode led the Clinton's staff to reconsider the all server infrastructure setup due to limitation and security concerns and opted to move the server into a third party co-location environment for hosting. As highlighted in the FBI investigation, the successful bidder to host the "Pagliano" engineered Clinton's email server was a Denver based company "Platte River Network" or PNR which was maintaining a space in co-location facilities in New Jersey. In carrying out the planned hosting arrangement, an employee from PNR moved the server and supporting equipment into a secure data center in Secaucus, NJ run by Equinix. Subsequently, Clinton's server email accounts were migrated to the new server with added capabilities (i.e. Locally stored and cloud enabled backups) along with other accounts belonging to the domains presidentclinton.com, wjoffice.com and clintonemail.com. After this infrastructure migration, the old server Dell 1950 was disconnected or left idle in the co-location until it was acquired by the FBI in accord with Conolly & Williams the law firm representing the now former Secretary in the ensuing investigation relating to Clinton's email controversy.

The Blow Back

At this point, converging events began to create an environment of potential liability and vulnerability, or even compromise raising questions and concerns for Secretary Clinton in relation to her emails and supporting infrastructure. For example, in tidying up its paper work on different Secretaries of State, the DOS was asking questions to fill in its paperwork gaps from Madeline Albright, Colin Powell, Condoleezza Rice onto Hillary Clinton due to retention requirements. Equally, the US Congress had also began asking about documents related to Benghazi attacks that resulted in the death of US ambassador Chris Stevens. Surprisingly in checking, the folks at the DOS realized that they had never saved Clinton's emails, and moreover that she's been using a personal account from outside not an official one to conduct the Department business or diplomacy. Anticipating a potential record retention policy or law violation, the DOS asked Secretary Clinton to produce the relevant emails. Subsequently, the emails recovery tasks were undertaken by Clinton's personal lawyer Heather Samuelson, her aide Sheryl Mills along with the hosting company that migrated the server infrastructure. The relevant emails were then produced in part or whole for the Department of State and the House Benghazi committee also in process of investigating in the related matters.

By then in Dec 2014, Secretary Clinton and Ms. Abedin had changed again to a new domain hrcoffice.com and also turned over some 55,000 pages of emails along with about 30,490 separate emails to the State Department based on various evolving news accounts. Upon the review of the delivered emails by the DOS, it appeared that the unclassified emails also contained national security secrets. As result under scrutiny around this time in March 2nd 2015, the emails issues became a potential scandal for Clinton with a Headline by the New York Time "Hillary Clinton Used Personal Emails Account at State Department Possibly Breaking Rules". Consequently, the ensuing controversy would also trigger a subpoenaed by the House Select Committee on Benghazi seeking the relevant emails in the matter. Furthermore, the FBI would follow suit with its own investigation due to the referral from the Inspector General (IG) of the intelligence community based on potential evidence that Secretary Clinton's unusual email infrastructure might have led to the mishandling of classified materials. As if to underscore the disorganized management of the server infrastructure, the FBI reported 17,448 additional emails that had not been previously turned over by the Clinton's lawyer. The Pentagon also disclosed finding another set of 1,000 more emails between Clinton and Gen. David Petraeus. Moreover, in course of its investigation, the FBI recovered chains of emails that were either or should have been classified when the correspondences took place. Those emails correspondences were believed to include classified information from the DOS, CIA, FBI, NSA, NGA (National Geospatial Intelligence Agency) along with DOD.

The USIC and the FBI determined that 81 email chains on

Clinton's personal server system contained classified information from Confidential to Top Secret including Special Access Program believed to be the most sensitive between 2009 and 2013. In addition, the DOS determined based on its FOIA classification criteria that 2000 emails were classified Confidential and one (1) as Secret.

Ultimately, the scandal or controversy relating to the emails impacted Clinton in terms of at least unwelcomed news coverages, the related ensuing investigation by the FBI and perhaps her chances of becoming President of the United States in 2016 election against Donald Trump. In essence, it can be argued that we will never conclusively know how many successful hacks occurred against the Clinton's email infrastructure since some front end devices owned or used by Secretary Clinton were not recovered and examined as highlighted in the FBI report.

Concluding Analysis

Notwithstanding the controversy underpinnings such as the ongoing news coverages, the attempted or successful hackings and the unusually engineered Clinton's emails infrastructure, there was only one and direct compromise of the server via cyber intrusion acknowledged by the FBI in its report. Moreover, the indirectly successful hack via spear phishing including other methods was done leveraging a third party email by Guccifer. Arguably, other major contributing factors were in part rooted in the DOS own lax security culture at the time and prior toward information handling which was illustrated by the FBI and other investigative news outlet reporting as well. Contextually, the security awareness should be an ongoing mitigation tool in a more comprehensive risk management framework for protecting the DOS assets.

The appearance of attempting to circumvent the laws or the required DOS operational security measures by the actors involved, may have cast doubts which should be resolved at this point as judgment calls on the part of potential readers or observers. The inability by the FBI to conclusively state that all the potential compromises had been accounted for is due in some measure to missing devices and their contents along with the presence of classified information on an unclassified system in giving a fair public hearing in this email controversy.

References

AP (2016, August 29). FBI: No evidence Clinton server hacked despite Trump tweet. AP News. Retrieved from https://www.apnews.com/380b995c9fd94e03b09e6c0fcacf1 0

23

Gass, N. (2016, Sept 2). Powell warned Clinton about using Blackberry. Politico. Retrieved from https://www.politico.com/story/2016/09/clinton-blackberry-colin-powell-227691

Gerstein, J. (2016, Sept 13). Ex-Hillary Clinton aide refuses to appear at email hearing. Politico. Retrieved from https://www.politico.com/story/2016/09/clinton-aide-no-show-email-hearing-228090

Collinson, S. and Kopan, T. (2016, July 6). FBI director: Hillary Clinton 'extremely careless' but no charges recommended. CNN. Retrieved from https://www.cnn.com/2016/07/05/politics/fbi-director-doesnt-recommend-charges-against-hillary-clinton/index.html

Weiner, R. and Hsu, S. (2016, Sept 1). Hacker known as Guccifer sentenced to 52 months in prison. The Washington Post. Retrieved from https://www.washingtonpost.com/local/public-safety/guccifer-hacker-who-revealed-clintons-use-of-a-private-email-address-sentenced-to-52-months/2016/09/01/4f42dc62-6f91-11e6-8365-b19e428a975e_story.html?utm_term=.39c49e6e6d6e

13

UBER

By: Tom Devore

Uber, the biggest ride share company in the world was compromised in March 2016. The attack on Uber is an interesting case not necessarily because of the method of attack or the individuals committing the act. But, what makes this case so interesting is how poor Uber handled the incident, which resulted in serious legal ramifications and a tarnished reputation that the company has had to overcome.

In October 2016, two unidentified cyber hackers were able to breach Uber's computer servers and they stole personal data from more than 57 million customers and employees. The hackers demanded $100,000 in exchange for deleting the stolen data. Uber reportedly paid the hackers and it's assumed that the stolen data was destroyed since there were no signs of fraud or misuse. According to Bloomberg, who first broke the news, the information that the cyber criminals were able to obtain was names, email addresses, and phone numbers of customers. The hackers also were able to get over 600,000 driver's license numbers of drivers that were employed by Uber. Uber reports that more sensitive data such as credit card information, banking accounts, and social security numbers were not compromised. It wasn't until November 2017 that Uber released the details about the incident. (Kleinman, 2017)

To make matters worse, they attempted to conceal the breach and theft of data from the public as well neglecting to notify law enforcement authorities. Uber paid the $100,000 secretly through a bug bounty account. The bug bounty is a program that many of the major tech companies use to pay people who are able to find vulnerabilities in their network so that the companies can correct their security deficiencies (Hogg, 2018).

It was also discovered that the company's chief executive officer at the time of the incident, Travis Kalanick, knew about the breach from the beginning and held onto the information for over a year. As per federal and state law, they were required to disclose any significant data breaches to regulators and it took over a year for Uber to report the incident. (Larsen, 2017)

Federally, the Securities and Exchange Commission (SEC) is the federal agency tasked with enforcing the statutory requirement for public companies, and, in October 2011, the SEC issued a non-binding disclosure guidance regarding the reporting obligations for public companies in reference to significant cyber incidents and Cybersecurity Risks. In terms of state laws regarding disclosing cyber-crimes, there are several states that require all companies disclose any security incidents or issues that involve breaches or hackings. These states include California and New York, which have both initiated their own investigation in regards to the incident.

The cover-up was not an isolated incident; Uber was already under investigation by the Federal Trade Commission (FTC) for the same type of deceptive behavior. The investigation revolved around another security breach that occurred in 2014 in which Uber failed to disclose an unrelated data breach.

The incident caused a major shake-up in the Uber organization and the dismissal of top executives. Travis Kalanick, who was the co-founder of Uber, resigned in June 2017 as the result of covering-up the incident as well as various other high profile scandals that had occurred in the last couple years. It was reported by Bloomberg that Kalanick was aware of the hacking and that he was instrumental in attempting to conceal the incident from the public. Uber's security chief executive, Joe Sullivan, was also dismissed from the company. Sullivan was a former federal prosecutor who specialized in criminal cyber cases, as well having held top security positions with Ebay and Facebook. Sullivan was replaced by John Flynn, who was previously employed by Google and was credited with the development of their intrusion detection group. Also, three of Sullivan's security staff was terminated due to the incident. They were the chief of staff of the security department, Pooja Ashok, a senior security engineer, Prithvi Rai, and Jeff Jones, who handled physical security. (Kleinman, 2017)

Dara Khosrowshahi assumed the CEO position after Kalanick's dismissal. He has acknowledged the mismanagement of this incident and made it a point to assure the public that Uber is committed to correcting their mistakes. Khosrowshahi stated that "None of this should have happened, and I will not make excuses for it. While I can't erase the past, I can commit on behalf of every Uber employee that we will learn from our mistakes." In regard to the information stolen, Khosrowshahi is confident that information is not in jeopardy. He said, "While we have not seen evidence of fraud or misuse tied to the incident, we are monitoring the affected accounts and have flagged them for additional fraud protection." Uber has retained the former general counsel at the National Security Agency, Matt Olsen, as a cybercrime legal adviser, and has contracted Mandiant, an outside security firm, to investigate the security breach. Uber said Olsen stated that he intends to reorganize the Uber's security team. (Kleinman, 2017)

On February 6, 2018, the new chief information security officer, John Flynn, testified on Capitol Hill on Uber's behalf. The testimony was to the Senate Commerce Consumer Protection, Product Safety, Insurance and Data Security Subcommittee and he had to answer for the Breach and cover-up. Flynn testified that "Uber had made mistakes", including disguising the payment to the hackers through its bug bounty program. Flynn also stated that Uber made contact with the hackers and received "assurances" the stolen data was destroyed before they received the $100,000 payment. In December of 2016, a security team conducted a forensic analysis of the hacker's computer to verify the deletions. Senator Jerry Moran commented on the incident by saying "The fact that the company took approximately a year to notify impacted users raises red flags within this committee as to what systemic issues prevented such time-sensitive information from being made available to those left vulnerable," Democratic Senator Richard Blumenthal said Uber was "morally wrong and legally reprehensible," (Volz, 2018)

Who committed the crime

According to the Bloomburg, Uber's security executives know the identity of the hackers. Reports indicate that there were two individuals involved in the hacking incident. Reuters reported in December that the primarily perpetrator was a 20 year old male from Florida. The second individual was male from Canada. The Canadian male was apparently the one who demanded the payment and amount. Flynn confirmed the two male's involvement at the Senate Commerce Consumer Protection, Product Safety, Insurance and Data Security Subcommittee testimony on Capitol Hill. (Volz, 2018)

How the crime occurred.

The crime was financially motivated and wasn't conducted in a sophisticated manner. The hackers broke into the accounts of two Uber engineers on a coding site called Github. The hackers accessed a private area of the Github site and that's where they found Uber's log-in credentials to Amazon Web Services. AWS is a cloud computing service used by companies to store data. That's where they were able to obtain the passwords to an online data storage that contained the personal info which was stored unencrypted. According to the Bloomberg report, Uber did not provide precise details of the actual crime and it is unknown which countries outside the US had been affected by the hack. (Larsen, 2017)

What where the ramifications.

One could argue that another possible ramification from this incident could be that the company may be more of a target since a large sum of money was paid to the hackers. The company may be perceived as an easy target for potential hackers who think that they'll pay them off if they launch an attack. Many cyber experts felt that by the initial ransom was a mistake, and that it sent a message that they will pay for bad behavior. (ISACC, 2017)

How it could have been avoided.

This incident could have been prevented if the customer's and driver's data stored in the company's server were encrypted. Encryption is mainly used on the internet to protect information and is considered one of the most important methods for providing data security. It functions by sending sensitive data such as passwords, banking information, credit card numbers, and other personal information, converting that data from plaintext to an encoded version that can only be decoded by an authorized entity that has access to a decryption key. The encryption process is designed to provide data protection from end to end while it's transmitted across networks. The data on Uber's server was not encrypted; therefore the information stored was left vulnerable. (Rouse, 2017)

What are the lessons learned from the crime.

Uber learned some very painful lessons from this incident which directly impacted them financially as well as casting a dark shadow on their reputation. The company now has a very serious public relation problems which will most likely follow them for the foreseeable future. The personnel changes as well as policy changes shows that they're committed to improving their security standards and transparency. Recently a resource page for the drivers affected by the breach has been set up. Also, the drivers have been offered free credit monitoring protection. Unfortunately, the customers affected are not yet receiving any monitoring protection or any other resources. (Wong, 2017)

References

Cadwaladar. (2017, Sep. 18). Equifax Data Breach Highlights SEC
  Disclosure Obligations for Public Companies in the Wake of
  Cybersecurity Attacks. Retrieved from
  https://www.cadwalader.com/resources/clients-friends-
  memos/equifax-data-breach-highlights-sec-disclosure-
  obligations-for-public-companies-in-the-wake-of-
  cybersecurity-attacks

Isacc, M. Benner, K., & Frenkel, S.(2017, Nov. 21). Uber hid 2016
  breach, paying hackers to delete stolen data. *The New York
  Times.* Retrieved from
  https://mobile.nytimes.com/2017/11/21/technology/uberha
  ck.html?utm_content=buffereedae&utm_medium=social&ut
  m_source=twitter.com&utm_campaign=buffer

Kleinman, Z. (2017, June 21). Uber: The scandals that drove Travis
  Kalanick out. *BBC News.* Retrieved
  from http://www.bbc.com/news/technology-40352868

Larsen, S. (2017, Nov. 23). Uber's massive hack: What we know.
  Cnn.tech. Retrieved from
  http://money.cnn.com/2017/11/22/technology/uber-hack-
  consequences-cover-up/index.html

Lee, D. (2017, Nov. 22). Uber concealed huge data breach. BBC
  News. Retrieved from http://fimuko.com/assets/pawel-cv.pdf

Rouse, (Nov. 2017), TechTarget. Encryption. Retrieved from
  https://searchsecurity.techtarget.com/definition/encryption

Volz, D. (2018, Feb. 6). Uber says hackers behind 2016 data breach were in Canada, Florida. *Reuters.* Retrieved from https://www.reuters.com/article/us-uber-cyber-congress/uber-says-hackers-behind-2016-data-breach-were-in-canada-florida-idUSKBN1FQ2YO

Wong, J.C. (2017, Nov. 22). Uber concealed massive hack that exposed data of 57m users and drivers. The guardian. Retrieved from https://www.theguardian.com/technology/2017/nov/21/uber-data-hack-cyber-attack

Hogg,J.J. (2018, Mar. 7), Cyber hacks driving 'bug bounty' jobs and programs in corporate. *America, FoxBusiness.* Retrieved from https://www.foxbusiness.com/features/cyber-hacks-driving-bug-bounty-jobs-and-programs-in-corporate-america

14

YAHOO

By: Dana Tannatt

On September 22, 2016, Yahoo admitted to a breach that occurred in 2014 that compromised 500 million user accounts. At the time this was considered one of the largest breaches in history. This was discovered after law enforcement approached Yahoo after finding information on the dark web for sale that contained large amounts of personal data believed to be from Yahoo account holders. This was verified by Yahoo to be accurate. At this time Yahoo was convinced that this was the work of a nation state and not individual hackers acting alone (Goel & Perlroth, 2016).

The breach compromised personal information that spanned not only the Yahoo.com sites but also other Yahoo properties such as Tumblr, a popular social media platform, and Flickr, an image hosting site. The personal information included user account names, email addresses, telephone numbers, dates of birth, encrypted passwords and encrypted and unencrypted security questions. Yahoo ensured the media that unprotected passwords, credit/debit card data and bank account information was not compromised in any way and any critical sensitive information was safe (Daily Mail, 2017).

Just three months later December 14, 2016, Yahoo announces that in 2013 there was another breach that compromised 1 billion Yahoo accounts. This at the time was the largest breach ever recorded. Yahoo confirmed as it did in the previous report that the breach did not include any critical sensitive data and was restricted to the same type of information it reported in their previous report. Even without compromising critical sensitive information, the danger is still present. The risk is that many users may use the same account name structure across their online presence. The information exposed in these breaches can be used in targeted emails by hackers to trick users into giving up additional information that could expose their most critical online assets (Goel & Perlroth, 2016).

Yahoo did notify all account holders that their information may have been compromised and suggested steps like changing their password and to lookout for email scams to attempt to gather additional information (Goel & Perlroth, 2016). In late 2016 Yahoo took action for those who did not respond to their recommendations and forces a password change for all accounts, thus invalidating any compromised security questions and answers (Selyukh, 2017).

All of this information was being released during a critical time for Yahoo. They were under negotiations for a merger with Verizon worth at the time $4.8 billion dollars (Goel & Perlroth, 2016).   This forced Verizon to reassess the merger and perform some investigation into the breach and renegotiation on the terms of the merger (Goel & Perlroth, 2016). Even though the merger was finalized in June of 2017 at a discount of $350 million resulting in a $4.48 billion sale, Verizon continued its investigation into the breach of 2013 using an outside auditing firm. After the investigation the breach that thought to affect 1 billion, Yahoo admitted in October of 2017, that the 2013 breach affected all 3 billion of its accounts at that time. Thus, cementing it as the largest breach ever (Daily Mail, 2017).

An update in November 2017 a Canadian man, Karim Baratov, pleaded guilty to conspiracy to commit computer fraud and abuse and eight counts of aggravated identity theft. Baratov is pleading guilty to hacking at least 11,000 webmail accounts. Authorities further confirmed that Baratov was being directed by two Russian intelligence agents. The two Russian intelligence agents working for the Russian Federal Security Service or FSB contacted Baratov through Russian language hacker for hire websites. Baratov used spearfishing emails, a tactic to target specific users and trick them into visiting sites that seemed legitimate and asked for credentials that could be used gather information on those users. He would send screen shots to the FSB to prove he had achieved the hack and collect payment. Baratov willingly went to the US for a hearing and claimed he did not know he was working for Russian agents connected to the breach. The two Russian agents Dmitry Dokuchaev and Igor Sushchin used the information they stole from the Yahoo breach to spy on Russian journalists, US and Russian government officials and employees of financial services and other private businesses. Due to the lack of an extradition treaty with Russia these FSB agents will probably never be tried for their crimes.

References

Goel, V. and Perlroth, N. (2016, Dec). Yahoo Says 1 Billion User Accounts Were Hacked. The New York Times. Retrieved from https://www.nytimes.com/2016/12/14/technology/yahoo-hack.html

Daily Mail. (2017, Nov). 'Hacker-for-hire' pleads guilty to charges stemming from Yahoo! Breach which affected half a billion user accounts and was 'directed by Russian intelligence agents'. Associated Press. Retrieved from http://www.dailymail.co.uk/news/article-5127005/Hacker-hire-pleads-guilty-Yahoo-breach.html

Selyukh A. (2017, Oct). Every Yahoo Account That Existed In Mid-2013 Was Likely Hacked. National Public Radio. Retrieved from https://www.npr.org/sections/thetwo-way/2017/10/03/555016024/every-yahoo-account-that-existed-in-mid-2013-was-likely-hacked

15

LINKEDIN

By: Jonathan Lancelot

Imagine being an unemployed job seeker with limited funds to make ends meet. Entrusting a social networking platform with important and sensitive information, and your account password combination has been compromised, opening up data assets to theft and sale on the dark web. This happened on May 17, 2016: A 2012 data breach came back to haunt LinkedIn when

117 million email and password combinations stolen by hackers four years ago popped up online. At the time the breach occurred, members who had been affected were told to reset their passwords. That information then became publicly available in May 2016. LinkedIn acted quickly to invalidate passwords of all LinkedIn accounts that were created prior to the 2012 breach and had not undergone a reset since the breach. It is not clear who stole the information or published it online, but LinkedIn is actively working with law enforcement officials. LinkedIn hack hits the headlines — for a second time. If 2016 was anything, it was the year of the repeatedly broken records. LinkedIn was the first of many hack records that were met (and later surpassed) this year. The business networking company was first hit in 2012, but the scale of the attack was only realized this year when the number of records stolen shot up by almost twenty-fold to 117 million accounts. If that wasn't bad enough, most of the passwords were ridiculously bad -- like "123456" and "LinkedIn." The alleged hacker was eventually caught in the Czech Republic, yet the damage was done.

LinkedIn was lacking a proper cyber-defense strategy and risked critical systems, their reputation, and legal jeopardy. The company made a public statement saying "we became aware that data stolen from LinkedIn in 2012 was being made available online. This was not a new security breach or hack. We took immediate steps to invalidate the passwords of all LinkedIn accounts that we believe might be as risk. These were accounts created prior to the 2012 breach that had not reset their passwords since that breach" (LinkedIn). The lesson to be learned here is what happened, and how can an organization guard against a cyber-attack of this nature? LinkedIn could have been a target of social engineering as the "company was the victim of unauthorized access and disclosure of some members' passwords.

At the time, our immediate response included a mandatory password reset for all accounts we believed were compromised as a result of the unauthorized disclosure" (Press Association). Even though how the unauthorized disclosure unfolded is elusive, we can deduce that some form of elicitation took place, exposing the companies critical systems to a cyber-attack. "Elicitation means to bring or draw out, or arrive at a conclusion" (Hadnagy, page. 55), in this case, it could have drawn out an employee to divulged sensitive information that has the hacker an opening to steal data. In other words, elicitations expose vulnerabilities for the hacker to exploit. One could argue the exploit was a zero-day as the vulnerability was unknown. A zero-day "is a nasty little bug that exploits vulnerabilities in existing systems that are known only to the hacker" (Moschovitis, page. 107). When the cyber-attack was executed, the results were devastating. Again, we can only speculate to who, what, when, where, and how.

Nevertheless, we can view the aftermath of an attack, observe its severity, and narrow down the means of how it was done, and what was not done. "The goal with zero-day exploits is simple: Stay alert, stay informed, and have in place a defense-in-depth strategy that protects your organization as much as is practical" (Moschovitis, page. 107). In this case, LinkedIn learned the hard way, and millions were affected.

Hindsight is 20/20, yet it is essential that we recognize factors that could have prevented LinkedIn's critical assets from being compromised. First, Vulnerability identification and testing could prevent a catastrophic cyber-attack, human and computer networking factor correspondingly. In the realm of detective controls, a 'defense-in-depth approach would have saved millions of users and the company the despondency of data loss. "The right way to use detective, corrective, and compensatory controls is by deploying the, across systems in a way that achieves defense-in-depth. This has the effect of putting multiple and diverse barriers between the attack and the asset" (Moschovitis, page. 135). These barriers should be encryption walls or other controls that makes asset penetrations difficult if not impossible if the intruder manages to enter the network.

Most importantly, the human factor (which could be the issue in this case) applies when we are deliberating control methods within the context of cyber-security and risk management. Again, the people component is the most critical element of a successful cybersecurity program. Support from the board on down is crucial. This support must be emphatic, clear, and actionable. There can be no doubt anywhere in the company that cybersecurity is a mission-critical organizational practice: It needs to be supported with clear policies, standards, procedures, and guidelines" (Moschovitis, page.137). We can deduce that LinkedIn was not prepared to the degree that has been stated here, and it is a difficult lesson to learn for a company entrusted with the critical data of millions of clients. It is even more difficult for an individual whose expectation is a total defense of their information as they seek the next employer only to find their data is in the hands of a cybercriminal on the dark web.

References

Hadnagy, C. (n.d.). *Social Engineering: The Art Human Hacking*.

Indianapolis, IN: Wiley Publishing.

LinkedIn. (2016, May). Notice of Data Breach: May 2016. Retrieved

March 13, 2019, from

www.linkedin.com/help/linkedin/answer/69603/notice-of-data-

breach-may-2016?lang=en

Moschovitis, C. (2018). *Cybersecurity Program Development for Business: The Essential Planning Guidey*. Hoboken, NJ: John Wiley and Son Publishing.

Press Association. (2016, May 18). Hacker advertise details of 117 million LinkedIn users on darknet. Retrieved from www.theguardian.com/technology/2016/may/18/hacker-advertises-details-of-117-million-linkedin-users-on-darknet

16

IRS

By: Jonathan Lancelot

On February 29, 2016, the Internal Revenue Service (IRS) announced that the data breach they uncovered in May 2015 was much more significant than initially believed. In May, the IRS said over 100,000 American taxpayers had their personal information compromised when the agency's "Get Transcript" system was hacked. However, in February 2016, those numbers have been increased to over 700,000. The IRS thinks a sophisticated Russia-based criminal operation is responsible for the data breach and that identities were stolen to file fraudulent tax returns in the future. This is not only a danger to the critical systems holding the nations confidential and top secret assets; it is a danger to national security and the American public-at-large. On the international scale, the cybercrimes should be seen as an act of cyber-warfare, and let the Russian diplomats do all the work to prove it was not, and it was some rogue criminal organization, a non-state actor within the Russian border — the attribution problem, meaning pinpointing the source of the cyber-attack, and its associated identity. US cyber-diplomatic policy would have to press a rapprochement as long as a reasonable doubt can prove that an act of war did not take place. The next determination would be the cyber-attack is an act of cyber-terrorism or a cybercrime. The asset of the federal government asset cover "more than 900,000 separate real assets covering more than 3 billion sq.ft, mineral rights, on and offshore, covering 2.515 billion acres of land, more than the total surface land of Canada, 45,190 underutilized buildings, the operating costs of which are $1.66 billion annually, and Oil and gas resources on an offshore worth $128 trillion, roughly eight times the national debt of the country" (Matthews). The valuation of the US digital assets is elusive as "federal government data plays a large role in the American economy, but this role has been obscured because it is difficult to measure the value of information" (Brantley). Despite the difficulty in valuation, the information held by the Federal government is a matter of national security.

The critical systems of the IRS were penetrated as there was no barrier or encryption wall to keep hackers away from information assets. "The criminals were especially after E-file PINs, which are used by some individuals to file returns electronically, the agency said in a statement released Tuesday. Around 464, 000 unique social security numbers (SSN) were involved, and of the total, 101,000 SSNs were used to successfully access an E-file PIN" (Chew). The IRS had a defense-in-depth control scheme that let the thieves in so far. "The cybercriminals used personal taxpayer data that was stolen elsewhere to help generate the PINs, the agency said. No personal data was compromised or disclosed by IRS systems, and affected taxpayers will be notified by mail of the attack" (Chew). In this case, we would have to take the government's word that has a risk management plan in place as this was not the first time, yet how does one audit the federal government regarding its cyber-defense strategy? In other words, what recourse does a taxpayer have in finding out if their personal data was stolen during a cyber-attack on government computer networks? Not much.

"This attack followed a massive data breach at the IRS in 2015, when hackers stole information from 330,000 taxpayers (other later reports said 724,000 taxpayers) to successfully file bogus tax refunds and obtain $50 million in federal funds" (Chew), a disaster in trust between citizens and the government institution that requires personal data for the purpose of paying taxes, a requirement a taxpayer has no legal say. Despite the reputational risk to the IRS scope of service and the system used in processing tax funds, the legal supremacy of the Federal government remains intact, and the citizens are left in the space of doubt and powerlessness in how their data is protected unless their representative in the United States Congress has the political will to take up the cause. "Due to their nature, position, and size, federal networks need stronger security measures than most organizations. So far the cybersecurity resources devoted are not in proportion with the risk" (Kshetri). Congress passed a law "after eight years of discussion. The Cybersecurity Act of 2015 was Division N of the omnibus spending bill that was enacted by Congress. Title I of the bill was the information sharing provision" (Rosenzweig). It remained to be seen if the legislation would be enough to defend critical government system against cybercriminals, cyber terrorist, rogue states, and hacktivist organizations. "Government spending on cybersecurity, fighting cybercrimes has also increased" (Kshetri), and will increase exponentially for years to come.

President Obama reacted to the 2015 and the 2016 attacks as "the White House released the Cybersecurity National Action Plan. It includes a multifaceted cybersecurity effort within the federal government, extended through the private sector and even with recommendations for individual behavior to improve personal security" (Kshetri). Still yet, the government sector has to beware of data breaches that can compromise national security. As minor as it could seem that taxpayer PINs were stolen from IRS, and a quick fix implemented, the implication for national security remain as the federal government will continue to be the target of elaborate, well planned, and crippling cyber-attacks. The American people have a responsibility to pay taxes to the government, and that requires the taxpayer to give personal information that can be used against them in the wrong hands. It is the responsibility for the government to uphold its end of the arrangement by safeguarding taxpayer information just as if they are protecting information on top-secret subjects that require levels of barriers and walls to fortify successfully.

References

Brantley, B. (2018, March 14). The Value of Federal Government

Data. Retrieved from digital.gov/2018/03/14/data-breifing-value-

federal-government-data/

Chew, J. (2016, February 10). The IRS Says Identity Thieves Hacked Its

Systems Again. *Fortune Magazine*. Retrieved from

fortune.com/2016/02/10/irs-hack-refunds/

Kshetri, N. (2016, February 16). Why the IRS Was Hacked Again and

What the Feds Can Do About It. *US News*. Retrieved from

www.usnews.com/news/article/2016-02-16/why-the-irs-was-

hacked-again-and-what-the-feds-can-do-about.it

Matthews, C. (2013, February 05). The Federal Government's $128

Trillion Stockpile: The Answer to Our Deft Problems. *Time*.

Retrieved from business.time.com/2013/02/05/the-federal-

governments-128-trillion-stockpile-the-answer-to-our-debt-

problems/

Rosenzweig, P. (2015, December 16). The Cybersecurity Act of

2015. *LawFare*. Retrieved March 13, 2019, from

lawfareblog.com/cybersecurity-act-2015

17

CONCLUSION

While 2016 was a year of many firsts, it will be defined by the cyber security incidents of the Presidential election. Both the Russian interference and Mrs. Clinton's email controversy brought cyber security to the front page of America's newspapers. Hopefully these incidents also raised awareness among the population and caused people to take a serious look at their own cyber security habits.

You may have noticed a recurring theme in the book, that many of these attacks could have been avoided. CEO of FireEye, Kevin Mandia said, "persistent hackers are exploiting human trust and not exploiting systems" and it is often said that humans are the weakest link in cyber security. These incidents certainly support that hypothesis.

The important lessons to take away from these incidents: Use security verification questions with personal information that is not easily discovered such as a favorite teacher; Set up two factor authentication where available; And do not mix business and personal email.

Thank you very much for purchasing our book, we truly appreciate it. We hope you enjoyed it and learned a little about the serious threat hackers pose to every person and business.

ABOUT THE EDITORS

Thomas Hyslip is currently the Resident Agent in Charge of the Department of Defense, Defense Criminal Investigative Service (DCIS), Cyber Field Office, Eastern Resident Agency. Prior to joining the DCIS in 2007, Dr. Hyslip was a Special Agent with the US Environmental Protection Agency, Criminal Investigation Division, and the US Secret Service. Throughout his 20 years of federal law enforcement, Dr. Hyslip has specialized in cybercrime investigations and computer forensics. Dr. Hyslip has testified as an expert witness on computer forensics and network intrusions at numerous federal, state, and local courts.

Dr. Hyslip is currently a faculty member at Norwich University within the Master of Science in Information Security & Assurance program. Dr. Hyslip received his Doctor of Science degree in Information Assurance from Capitol College in 2014. Dr. Hyslip previously obtained a Master of Science degree from East Carolina University and a Bachelor of Science degree from Clarkson University. Dr. Hyslip holds numerous industry and government certification including the Certified Ethical Hacker (C|EH), NSA-IAM, and SCERS from the Federal Law Enforcement Training Center.

Rosemarie A. Pelletier is the program director for the Master of Public Administration and Master of Science in Information Security & Assurance programs at Norwich University. Dr. Pelletier has several years of experience in education, public policy, and real estate. She has been teaching in Virginia for 15 years in the classroom and for about 10 years online, where she wrote and developed courses and chaired dissertation committees. Dr. Pelletier was the president and founder of a company responsible for the identification, research, and development of projects suitable for construction by the formation of a public-private partnership.

Dr. Pelletier served as the Secretary of the Virginia State Technology Council where she advised the Executive and Legislative branches on technology policy issues. She chaired the Transportation Technology Advisory Panel in writing the Transportation Technology Blueprint for the Commonwealth of Virginia. She was appointed by Governor George Allen to the Joint

Committee on Technology and Science to study and advise on technology and science policies. Appointed by Governor Mark Warner, Dr. Pelletier served on the statewide speakers bureau to address transportation funding issues throughout the Commonwealth. She combines her knowledge and experience in technology policy with her education in public policy and public administration to bring the best of both worlds to Norwich University.

At George Mason University, she earned her Bachelor of Arts in English and Philosophy, her MPA, and began her Ph.D. work. She then went on to the University of Baltimore to receive her Doctorate in Public Administration, specializing in policy and project implementation.

George J. Silowash was named Chief Information Security Officer (CISO) for Norwich University in December 2016. Previously, he was a cybersecurity threat and incident analyst within the CERT® at the Software Engineering Institute (SEI), a unit of Carnegie Mellon University. He has over a decade of experience in the information technology field, including systems administration and information security. His latest work involves developing technical controls using open source software to counter data exfiltration attempts by malicious insiders. Other areas of interest include privacy and security, digital forensic investigations, and critical infrastructure security. Before joining CERT, he was an Information Systems Security Officer for the United States Department of Justice, National Drug Intelligence Center. He was also a systems administrator for a healthcare company prior to working in the Federal government. He holds a master of science in information assurance from Norwich University and is a certified information systems security professional (CISSP).

www.ingramcontent.com/pod-product-compliance
Lightning Source LLC
Chambersburg PA
CBHW051244050326
40689CB00007B/1061